One West,
Two Myths

A Comparative Reader

One West, Two Myths

A Comparative Reader

Edited by C. L. Higham and Robert Thacker

University of Calgary Press

Canada Canada Council   Conseil des Arts
        for the Arts   du Canada

We acknowledge the financial support of the Government of Canada
through the Book Publishing Industry Development Program
(BPIDP) for our publishing activities. We acknowledge the support
of the Alberta Foundation for the Arts for this published work.

The University of Calgary Press gratefully acknowledges the Donner
Canadian Foundation for its support of this publication.

National Library of Canada Cataloguing in Publication

One west, two myths : a comparative reader / edited by C.L.
Higham and Robert Thacker.

Includes bibliographical references and index.
ISBN 1-55238-135-8

1. Canada, Western--History. 2. West (U.S.)--History. I. Higham,
C. L. (Carol L.) II. Thacker, Robert

E179.5.O53 2004   971.2   C2004-902236-9

Printed and bound in Canada by AGMV Marquis

∞ This book is printed on 50% recycled, acid-free paper

Cover design by Mieka West
Page design and typesetting by Elizabeth Gusnoski

Contents

Acknowledgments

This volume and its related conference would have not been possible without help from the following people:

First, I must thank Robert Thacker of St. Lawrence University. Without his aid, encouragement, and vision, we could not have put together the conference and the subsequent volumes. Bob provided advice and confidence when I needed them. He helped recruit Robert Pickering of the Buffalo Bill Historical Center, who gave us a place for the first conference, grant writing skills *par excellence*, and enthusiasm. He, in turn, recruited Gerry Conaty of the Glenbow-Alberta Institute, who invited the conference to Calgary, helping us expand our reach and vision. Robert Pickering and Gerry Conaty wrote the grants that attracted the William H. Donner Foundation and the Donner Canadian Foundation. Their generosity underwrote the conference and this volume.

Several people were key to the creation of this volume. I owe Walter Hildebrandt, Joan Barton, and the Board of the University of Calgary Press for their patience and guidance. I would also like to thank the authors for their timely submissions and willingness to rewrite when necessary. Additionally, Paul Hirt of Washington State University provided guidance and permission for the project. Last, Derek and Rebecca Rodriguez of Davidson College gave me technical support as I fought with both scanners and Word.

Finally, I would like to thank my family. My parents, who helped babysit during the various conferences, and my husband, who encouraged me to pursue this idea and gladly took over a small child as I followed the conferences. Thank you to everyone for their help and support.

An Introduction to Comparing the Two Wests

C. L. Higham, Davidson College

What is comparative history? Why should anyone study it? Why compare Canada and the United States? Are they too similar (e.g., large English-speaking populations, dominant English heritage, etc.?) Or are they too different (e.g., Canada has Quebec, a smaller population, bigger land mass, etc.?) How can scholars and writers possibly compare their Wests? The United States had a violent frontier. Canada had a peaceful one.[1] The United States had cowboys; Canada had the Mounties. The United States has deserts. Canada has snow. Can we learn anything from comparing apples and oranges?

Think for a minute. When someone says "the United States," what comes to mind? When someone says "Canada," then what comes to mind? What do you think of when someone says "the West"? Is it an image of the United States or Canada that appears when the word "West" comes to mind? How do the images that come to mind represent one's knowledge about the subject? What do these images reveal about preconceptions?

Now a reader may disagree with the stereotypes presented above. That is precisely why one should think comparatively about history or about the world. By comparing two regions, experiences, nations, or peoples, one can learn about their similarities and their differences. Historian George Fredrickson defines comparative history as, "the systematic comparison of some process or institution in two or more societies that are not usually conjoined within one of the traditional geographical areas of historical specialization."[2] In the end, comparison helps historians better challenge conventionally held ideas about the groups being studied. Sociologist Seymour Martin Lipset puts it more succinctly; "Comparative analysis sometimes permits us to place a given result in contrast with a comparable event elsewhere."[3] Comparison confronts the beliefs that have become the status quo, the old guard, the establishment. It provides solid examples and data that can help refute misleading ideas based upon impressions. Myths, about our own countries and other countries, shape actions and policies. Comparative history challenges those myths.[4] In many ways, it can be a rebel force within the study of history.

A Brief History of Comparison

In his presidential address to the American Historical Association, Eric Foner discussed the importance of comparative history to future understandings of the United States' place in the world. He quoted Herbert Bolton's warning that treating American history in isolation would lead historians to help "raise up a 'nation of chauvinists.'"[5] Instead, Foner urged historians to broaden their understanding of their own histories. He stated "even histories organized along the lines of the nation-state must be, so to speak, deprovincialized, placed in the context of international interactions."[6] Coming on the crux of the twenty-first century, this cry sounded exciting and new. Yet as Foner pointed out, American history began as a comparative field and then drifted into "provincialism."[7]

Early historians of the United States and North America built their understanding of the "new" nations around their training and understanding of the "old" European ones. Francis Parkman's sweeping narratives of the settlement of the United States and Canada and William Prescott's discussion of the Spanish empire on the southern border, relied heavily on the histories and narratives of Europe. They grounded their understanding of the United States and Canada in how they differed from the traditional story of Europe.

The scientific historians, who followed them, looked for the opposite. They sought the similarities between the "established" histories of Europe and the "new" histories of Canada and the United States.[8] Eventually, with the rise of American studies, American history drifted away from comparison, except in two crucial fields: slavery and the frontier.[9]

The study of frontiers examines clashes of culture, social and political upheaval, and battles over resources. Frontiers, by definition, exist outside the realm of traditional European histories. They can occur in different areas of the world within a set time, aiding in comparison. Frontier comparative history breeds two sets of literature: those that discuss the value of comparison and those that compare the American or Canadian frontier to other regions of the world.[10]

In the last fifteen years, two unusual comparative works emerged. Howard Lamar's and Leonard Thompson's book, *The Frontier in History*, compared the South African frontier with the American western one. Both authors brought their expertise to bear on their particular region and then led the reader through the comparisons. It remains a unique work in the field. James Gump followed it five years later with an extension of the methodology. His work, *The Dust Rose Like Smoke* compares the Sioux war against the United States with the Zulu war against the British government in South Africa.[11] Lamar and Thompson focused on the broad trans-Mississippi West, illustrating a common criticism of comparative work: generalization. First, Lamar and Thompson infer that they will be examining the "North American" West, which would include Canada and Mexico. In reality, they focus on the United States trans-Mississippi West. Because Lamar and Thompson chose to compare all of the North American West, regional specialists can criticize their assumptions by pointing out regional exceptions. Narrowing the focus of the comparison, or defining the region or frontier in terms of how the actors defined them, as opposed to how current historians define them can offset this problem. Gump avoided this criticism as he defined the regions as the Sioux and Zulu did. This method, of course, invites the complaint that such narrowly defined regions are not representative. Or as George Fredrickson would say, "that [which] closely examines a particular community or social action in terms of conceptual schemes or categories that are applicable to the study of similar entities in other contexts."[12] Whether that is true or not, it certainly challenged conventional histories on United States Indian policy and South

Africa's Zulu War. It is comparative frontier histories such as these that led to this volume and its study of the frontiers of Canada and the United States.

WHY CANADA AND THE UNITED STATES?

Canada and the United States present the perfect case studies with which to begin or introduce comparative history. Seymour Martin Lipset pointed out years ago that "One of the most fruitful comparative approaches to American history has been one that emphasizes the ways in which the conditions facing new societies, new nations, and new or open frontiers have affected subsequent developments."[13] Canada represents an interesting counterpoint to the United States on those issues. Despite its continual political attachment to England, Canada and its peoples formed various new societies, encountered and defined frontiers, emerging as a unique nation.

On a more practical level, the comparison of Canada to the United States feeds into strongly held beliefs, often backed by inference or assumption. People in both Canada and the United States tend to possess preconceptions about the other group: they see only the similarities (they are like us because they speak English) or only see the differences (Canadians have socialized medicine but the United States does not.) The literature on both countries is accessible within each other's libraries and bookstores, making research for students easier. Topics can be chosen that only require one language (English), but bilingual projects exist as well. Most students know just enough about the opposing country to come to the field bearing preconceptions, which a project or which many lines of inquiry will reinforce or shatter and probably do a little of both.

The study of the West in Canada and the United States provides a unique laboratory for comparison. As Lipset has stated, frontiers or the perception of their existence, has shaped the history of the two countries. Traditionally, as several essays in the volume will demonstrate, or at least hint at, historians in Canada and the United States have viewed the development of their Wests differently. To begin with, Canadians often debate which is more significant within their history as a nation: their West or their North. This argument hinges on whether one conflates a western experience with a frontier one or sees them as fundamentally different.[14] Ray Allen Billington suggests that because the United States had a unique experience in their West, "the term 'frontier' has been endowed with a new meaning in the United States." He argues that Europeans, Asians, and Africans define the "frontier" in terms of "customs barriers, passport controls, and other troublesome hindrances to his freedom of movement." For Americans, Billington believes the term "frontier" implies "beckoning opportunity."[15] Billington assumes that Canadians use the European definition when defining their frontier.

Canadian historians do define their frontier development differently than U.S. historians do, but not necessarily in as static a manner as Billington suggests. Traditionally, Canadian historians view the evolution of their West through the prism of "metropolitanism" also known as the "hinterlands theory."[16] In a nutshell, this theory states that the markets of the metropolises in Europe and eastern Canada shaped the economic and political development of the hinterlands. In other words, the desires and needs of the established regions drove and defined the creation and development of the West and/or North in Canada. The significance of the fur trade in Canada represents the strongest example of this theory. This theory appears to fit Billington's characterization of European concepts of the frontier and explode it. On the one hand the frontier became a boundary for the companies and the urban areas. On the other hand the desires and needs created a "beckoning opportunity."

Historians in the United States have followed a different, older interpretation. In 1893, Frederick Jackson Turner announced, at the annual meeting of the American Historical Association, that the frontier was closed. He proceeded to present what became known as the "frontier thesis." His thesis revolved around the idea that the frontier or line between the civilized and uncivilized, settled and nomadic, organized and unorganized had ceased to exist, thus destroying the European concept of the frontier. Additionally, he argued that this frontier and the undeveloped areas beyond it made the United States unique in its development.[17] Significantly, Turner based his ideas not on the trans-Mississippi West (the area west of the Mississippi River) but rather on the first northwestern frontier that included Illinois, Kentucky, Wisconsin, etc. His evidence shaped his theory, though many later historians ignore that fact.[18] In the United States, the frontier thesis quickly shaped the field of Western history. It has come to revolve around at least two questions. Is the frontier a place or a process, a direct descendent of Turner's idea of a line between one group and another? Is the United States West unique or exceptional?

Both metropolitanism and the frontier thesis have come under attack over the years for being exclusionary of other groups and interpretations. And while their critics may have valid points, theories are meant to be tested. As Lipset points out, Turner "suggested the key aspect to understanding American society has been the way in which the experience of colonizing an open frontier resulted in individualism, egalitarianism, and strong political participation." But other countries, such as Canada and Australia, experienced open frontiers. Lipset goes on to say that Turner must be challenged in a "comparative context."[19] Comparing the two Wests or the various frontiers provides the perfect opportunity to test these ideas. How does the development of the United States West conform to the idea of metropolitan development? Under what conditions do certain aspects like trade and natural resource development appear to fit the hinterlands theory? On the other hand, United States historians might find their constant bickering about the frontier as place or process rechanneled if they apply it to Canada. Can the frontier be both a place and a process? If the market defines the frontier, then is it not a process? Or is it a place defined purely by where the resources stop and begin?

The question of American exceptionalism needs to be challenged within the context of Canadian/U.S. comparison. Both C. Vann Woodward and Eric Foner have pointed out that the American argument of exceptionalism creates pitfalls for historians. Woodward states that by laying claim "to distinctiveness and uniqueness in their national experience, to plead immunity from the influence of historical forces that have swept most other nations, to shun or deprecate comparisons between their history and that of other people, and to seek within their own borders all the significant forces that have shaped their histories" that American historians appear, in the eyes of other historians, to promote "narrow perspective and historical nationalism."[20] Foner demonstrates that even when writers have an understanding of the "global dimension of American history, ... their conviction that the United States represented a unique embodiment of the idea of freedom inevitably fostered a certain insularity."[21] The Canadian and United States Wests share many elements: native peoples, immigration from the interior, the east and the west, natural resources, cattle, wheat, mining, development of the Western metropolis, separation politics of the West, etc. So what exactly makes the United States West exceptional? Is it a cultural difference, a political difference? How do the similarities mask important differences? Is the Canadian West exceptional in its own way? Or are both Wests merely distinct?

Some comparative historians have tackled this issue by using regional identities to explore whether national identities or conceptions shape people's actions or perceptions. George Fredrickson argues that this is not comparative history. But he also admits that "there is no firm agreement on what a comparative history is or how it should be done."[22] The grandfather of these studies would be Paul Sharp's *Whoop-Up Country*. Sharp examined a region that revolved around the Canadian-United States border. He studied how historical actors and institutions used or ignored the border and national definitions in their business dealings across and along the border.

The relationship between the native populations and the non-native populations in Canada and the United States has become fertile ground for comparative works. From Roger Nichols's *Indians in the United States and Canada: A Comparative History* to Jill St. Germain's *Indian Treaty-making Policy in the United States and Canada, 1867–1877*, scholars attempt to better understand how two countries with similar conflicts with their indigenous peoples over land and natural resources resulted in different policies and solutions and similar modern conflicts.[23] How can an issue that was approached so differently produce very similar results?

The indigenous peoples of North America provide the perfect group with which to study comparative history. They did not see the national boundaries imposed by the European, American, and Canadian powers. They saw their own national boundaries. This different perspective forces historians to stop relying on traditional European definitions of nation-states. It also causes ethnohistorians and others to think beyond national identities and stories. As Eric Foner suggests, American historians, and Canadian historians as well, must avoid concentrating on their own nations.[24] By studying native peoples' perceptions of place and process, we gain a better understanding of how to approach comparison. Just because citizens of Canada and the United States shared similar backgrounds, legally, politically, and economically does not mean that they perceived the boundaries between regions and countries in similar ways. What do these differences tell us?

As the following essays will show, comparative thinking and study often presents one with multiple obstacles: everything from preconceptions about the validity of national boundaries to challenging long-held beliefs about motivating factors behind a country's history or the myths that bolster nationalist history.[25] Comparative history requires that the historian argue the case from multiple sides and embrace issues that are both confusing and fascinating. The differences of the two national cases can illuminate similarities while similarities can transcend differences. On the other hand, what are perceived to be similarities between regions, nations, or groups can suddenly appear radically different when examined side by side.[26]

In sum, these questions and others will be addressed, but maybe not completely answered, by the essays in this volume.

ESSAYS ON COMPARISON

This volume is not meant to provide a comprehensive view of Canadian and United States Western history. Nor is it designed to summarize or hand over the basic debates and arguments within the fields of Canadian and United States Western histories. Instead, it serves as an appetizer, a taste of what could come. But for the main course to follow, you must serve as the cook. Comparative history requires the energy and vision of youth. To be a comparativist, it is easier if one starts young, learning the skills that will be required for future studies.

The essays presented here represent three stages of how one studies Canada and the United States comparatively. The first essay addresses stereotypes and preconceptions that students and researchers may have about the two countries. Elliot West's piece shows how one must free one's mind to the multiple possibilities of what if? What if the boundaries between the United States and Canada ran vertically and geographically instead of horizontally? When we examine North America through those parameters, what questions arise? He then gives examples, with which one may agree or disagree, that explain areas of exploration for historians considering the United States and Canada.

The next two essays represent the standard beliefs about certain schools of history in Canada and the United States. Gerald Friesen lays out the argument about the modern, or what he calls the modern, myth of free trade in the late twentieth century, and how it shaped Canada and the United States. He lays out basic historical arguments presented by other authors and then muses on how those arguments fail when comparison is used. Donald Worster takes apart the myth that western Canada and the western United States developed differently, challenging future historians and writers to go deeper, back to the original sources that describe the re-carving of the North American continent into early, then mature modern nations. He suggests, as Foner and others have, that we must set aside the nationalist narratives and images that previous scholars have portrayed. These two essays help illustrate how "schools of thought," or dominant interpretations, can come to dominate a section of history, presenting a status quo that often is not or never challenged, even by emergent/beginning young historians.

The final five essays represent scholars using comparison to better understand how areas function as regions or nations outside the traditional historic boundaries of nations. They provide examples of how comparison can be used to explore issues of regionality versus nationality, individual versus national identity, and how processes and institutions change in different contexts or remain the same. They supply the raw materials for discussions of the promise and pitfalls of doing comparative history.

The first three essays use native peoples to reconceptualize the importance of the border between Canada and the United States. Beth LaDow studies how the Sioux and other native peoples saw the border as a "medicine line" that protected them from their respective enemies and pressures. The border bifurcated their traditional territories. As LaDow points out, while this division created problems, it also created new perceptions and opportunities for escape and refuge in opposing areas. Briefly, Indians fled from the United States to Canada and vice versa. Michel Hogue uses the Cree as his test of how Canadian and United States definitions of the border succeeded or failed. Though Canada and the United States chose the border and treated it as a physical entity, the Cree and their natural resource, the buffalo, did not. This rejection of the boundary line forced Canada and the United States to continually revisit their definition of the border *and* their definition of the people the border was meant to restrict.

McManus adds two more elements to the discussion of borders. While looking at how Canada and the United States redefined Blackfoot territory as their own, McManus adds two new elements: gender and cultural conceptions. She studies not just how the governments and native peoples view the boundary line but also how the settlers and different genders do. These essays introduce several questions, thanks to comparison. How do state defined conceptions of regions and borders clash with individual ones? How do people not included in nation-states view borders? How do overlapping definitions of frontiers and borders affect people? Who really defines borders and frontiers? What do the different responses of the nation-states and the native peoples tell us about their attitudes toward themselves and each other?

The last two essays look at regionality versus nationality. Molly Rozum's multilayered piece examines both how internal and external perceptions of a region shape the conception of that area for artists and writers. Her work clearly demonstrates that people with a relationship to the land see its nuances better than those who simply observe it from the outside or as they pass through. But she also raises questions about how definitions work in comparison. Peter Morris studies how borders function for individuals. Sometimes they are porous entities which individuals can ignore. In other cases individuals invoke the borders to protect individual interests. In either situation, they are not static. What do the terms "regions" and "regionality" mean versus "nation" and "nationality"? And when do individuals define themselves as such? All five of these authors represent the new generation of comparative scholars who seek to expand our knowledge of national and regional relationships.

The essays raise several questions, which will not be answered here but rather by future scholars. How do these scholars succeed in their comparisons? What do they leave unanswered? How can future scholars and researchers remedy these problems? What issues should be addressed by future comparative work?

Canada and the United States provide the most easily accessible case studies for introducing students in the United States and Canada to comparative history. But there is no need to stop there. With the proper language skills and grounding in history, many groups could be compared: Mexico and the United States, the English, French, and Spanish colonial empires in North America, or better yet, why not compare aspects of Canada, the United

States, *and* Mexico, for a truly North American perspective? How would our understanding of Native/non-Native relationships change if we examined them across the border in a comparative manner? What about women and their rights on the frontiers in Canada and the United States? How might that challenge our assumptions about women's roles within frontier and Western society? Numerous other topics come to mind: agricultural development, mining, forestry, water rights, Western marriage laws, racial tensions, immigrant experiences, the law and the gun, military movements ... and the list goes for as far as the eye can see. Add the case of Mexico as a counterweight, and the list becomes longer and more diverse. By being comparative, one also opens the door for issues that bleed across borders: intra-North American migration, intra-North American trade, natural resource production within North America (such as products that are raised in Mexico, processed in Canada, and sold to the United States). We might just find that North America experienced globalization far before the twenty-first century. Thus, while comparative history may not answer all questions, it certainly changes the questions themselves.

NOTES

1 For three examples, see Paul Sharp, *Whoop-Up Country: The Canadian and American West, 1865–1885* (Minneapolis: University of Minnesota Press, 1955); Seymour Martin Lipset, *Continental Divide: The Values and Institutions of the United States and Canada* (Middletown: Wesleyan University Press, 1982); Winks, *The Relevance of Canadian History* (Toronto: MacMillan of Canada, 1979).

2 George M. Fredrickson, "Comparative History," in Michael Kammen, ed., *The Past Before Us* (Ithaca: Cornell University Press, 1980), 458.

3 Seymour Martin Lipset, "The 'Newness' of the New Nation," in C. Van Woodward, ed., *The Comparative Approach to American History* (New York: Basic Books, 1968), 64.

4 Eric Foner, "Presidential Address: American Freedom in a Global Age," *The American Historical Review* 106, no. 1, February 2001, p. 1.

5 Hebert E. Bolton, *Wider Horizons of American History* (New York, 1939), p. 2, as cited in Eric Foner, "American Freedom in a Global Age," 3.

6 Foner, "American Freedom in a Global Age," 4.

7 Ibid., 1.

8 C. Vann Woodward, "The Comparability of American History," in C. Vann Woodward, ed., *The Comparative Approach to American History* (New York: Basic Books, 1968), 8–9.

9 Ibid., 11–15; George M. Fredrickson, "Comparative History," 462–63.

10 Pieces which simply talk about the importance of comparison include C. Vann Woodward's, *The Comparative Approach*; Michael Kammen's *The Past Before Us*; Peter Kolchin, "Comparing American History," *Reviews in American History* (December 1982), 64–81; Howard Lamar, "Coming into the Mainstream at last: comparative approaches to the history of the American West," *Journal of the West* 35, no. 4, October 1996, 3–5; Roger Adelson, "The U.S. West and Comparative History," *Journal of the West* 38, no. 2, April 1999, 3–7; Foner, "American Freedom in a Global Age."

11 Howard Lamar and Leonard Thompson, *The Frontier in History: North America and Southern Africa Compared* (New Haven, CT: Yale University Press, 1981); James O. Gump, *The Dust Rose Like Smoke: The Subjugation of the Zulu and the Sioux* (Lincoln: University of Nebraska Press, 1994).

12 Fredrickson, "Comparative History," 457.

13 Lipset, "The 'Newness' of the New Nation," 62.

14 Fredrickson, "Comparative History," 462.

15 Ray Allen Billington, "Frontiers," in C. Van Woodward, ed., *The Comparative Approach*, 76.

16 Harold Innis, *The Fur Trade in Canada: An Introduction to Canadian Economic History*, 1930, rev. ed. (Toronto: University of Toronto Press, 1956). For additional interpretations or applications of this theory see also, J. M. S. Careless, "Frontierism, Metropolitanism, and Canadian History," *Canadian Historical*

Review 35 (March 1954), 1–21; Donald Creighton, *The Commercial Empire of the St. Lawrence* (Toronto: Ryerson Press, 1937).

17 Frederick Jackson Turner, "The Significance of the Frontier in American History," *The Frontier in American History* (New York: H. Holt, 1920). For other interpretations, see Patricia Nelson Limerick, *The Legacy of Conquest: The Unbroken Past of the American West* (New York: W. W. Norton, 1987).

18 C. L. Higham, "Introduction – Turner in His Times and Ours," *Journal of the West* (1995), 5–6.

19 Lipset, "The 'Newness' of the New Nation," 69.

20 Woodward, "The Comparability of American History," 3.

21 Foner, "American Freedom in the Global Age," 7.

22 Fredrickson, "Comparative History," 457.

23 Roger Nichols, *Indians in the United States and Canada: A Comparative History* (Lincoln: University of Nebraska Press, 1998); Jill St. Germain, *Indian Treaty-Taking in the United States and Canada, 1867–1877* (Lincoln: University of Nebraska Press, 2001); C. L. Higham, *Noble, Wretched, and Redeemable: Protestant Missionaries to the Indians in Canada and the United States, 1820–1900* (Calgary: University of Calgary Press, 2000); Beth LaDow, *The Medicine Line: Life and Death on a North American Borderland* (New York and London: Routledge, 2001).

24 Foner, "American Freedom in the Global Age," 3.

25 Ibid.

26 Lipset, "The 'Newness' of the New Nation," 62.

Against the Grain:
State-Making, Cultures, and Geography
in the American West

Elliott West, University of Arkansas

Before we present to you matters of fact, it is fit to offer to your view the Stage where on they were acted, for Geography without history seemeth a carkasse without motion, [and] History without Geography wandereth as a vagrant without a certaine habitation. – John Smith, *The General History of Virginia*

Here's an experiment I have tried with my introductory American history survey. I give the class a physical map of North America. It shows landforms and vegetation, but no political boundaries. Do your best, I tell the students, to push out of your minds all the usual lines that show us nations, states, and provinces, all the cities and highways and railroads you expect to see on a standard map. It is 1491, I say, and you are seeing the continent freshly. Just look at the land, I tell them. Take in its shapes and its wrinkles, the flow of its rivers, its tilts and its grooves that lie this way and that. Now, I say, I'll tell you a secret and give you a job. Over the next few centuries, this continent will be organized into three nations. Your assignment is to speculate on what shape those nations will take. Given what you see, what will the political map look like?

I've gotten some strange and inventive answers, but most are consistent. One nation – we might call it Atlantis – hugs the eastern seaboard. It runs from around Hudson's Bay southward through the Maritime provinces and down the coastal plain to Florida. A second one, considerably larger, dominates the interior, and so we might name it Middle Earth. It includes Canada's plains provinces, the Mississippi watershed from the Appalachians to the Rockies, and Mexico's desert states from the Gulf to the Sierra Madre. The third nation might be called Greater Montana. It covers the continent's folded and uplifted western portion, the Canadian and U.S. Rockies and the Sierra Madre, the Sierra Nevada and coastal ranges, and the valleys and basins among the cordillera.

The imagined nations, falling naturally along geographical lines, reinforce what we ought to see all along. Atlantis, Middle Earth, and Greater Montana all run north and south because that is North America's natural geographical alignment. That in turn throws into sharp contrast the shape taken by events as we know they occurred. The three nations actually created, of course, run at right angles to the ones we've imagined. They run from coast to coast, east and west, against the continental grain. To put it another way, Canada, the United States, and Mexico don't make much geographical sense.

In John Smith's terms, the "matters of fact" seem to have stubbornly ignored the logic of the "Stage where on they were acted." The implications are considerable for all parts of North America, but especially for what we call the North American West. There we find the longest and most dramatic north-south geographical extensions, in our imagined Greater Montana and on the plains of Middle Earth. And those continuities run firmly across and counter to the national arrangements of Canada and the United States. Here, that is, the contradictions between landforms and nations seem the most glaring, which makes the West the obvious place to look for anything to learn from the odd pattern of modern state-making.

* * *

If anyone wonders whether we should expect historical and geographical patterns to overlap in the first place, North America's long past gives an undeniable answer. For most of continental history by far, human activity seems mostly to have followed the broad lay of the land. Assuming the earliest peoples migrated from what is now Siberia across the broad saddle of Beringia, they followed geographical contours southward. Archaeology of this earliest time suggests they moved down the Pacific shore and settled along the western edge of South America and probably on the California coast. Another route has them moving out of Alaska through a corridor between glacial sheets, travelling along the eastern face of the Canadian Rockies in a difficult passage that would empty them onto the plains where they could continue to the south, unimpeded and in the protective shadow of the mountains. These migratory patterns presumably produced some of the earliest human sites known, in coastal Chile and the many remains of the Clovis culture in the American Southwest.

Speculating on the movements of peoples over the next thousands of years is almost pure guesswork, but there are hints to be found in the arrangement among native groups when Europeans arrived. Language is an important key. We assume that people who speak similar languages were part of a common culture sometime in the past. At some point that culture broke apart and its components dispersed. If we mark indigenous groups on a map according to their language families, we can get some crude sense of their patterns of movement as they moved apart from each other. The result is striking. Five hundred years ago two of the seven most common language families – the Iroquoian (Iroquois Confederacy, Huron, Cherokee) and the Muskogean (Creek, Chickasaw, Choctaw) – were along a north-south axis in the eastern woodlands. A third, the Siouan, had a cluster of speakers on the south Atlantic coast (Catawba and Tutelo) but most lived in the Mississippi valley and the Great Plains (Dakota, Crow, Kansas, Osage, others) along another north-south axis that was also home to all peoples of a fourth family, the Caddoan (Caddo, Wichita, Arikara, Pawnee). The fifth and sixth language families were in the mountains and arid highlands stretching southward from Canada into Mexico – the Athapascan (Carrier, Chipewa, Dogrib, Hupa, Navajo, Apache, others) and the Uto-Aztecan (Bannock, Paiute, Shoshoni, Ute, Comanche, Hopi, Concho, Aztec).

The seventh family, the Algonkin, was a highly revealing exception to the general pattern. Some of these speakers were along the Atlantic coast (Abnaki, Micmac, Mohegan, Powhatan, others), some in the Great Lakes region (Illinois, Miami, Ojibwa, Ottawa, others), still others on the northern Great Plains (Cheyenne, Arapahoe, Blackfeet,[1] Cree, others). These peoples were aligned along North America's once prominent instance of an east–west geographical flow, the waterways of the St. Lawrence and Great Lakes and the easy watersheds beyond that, opening onto the Mississippi and Ohio River valleys and from there to the plains. In the seventeenth and eighteenth centuries this great opening through the Appalachian and forest barriers was used by the French to explode into the continental interior while the English remained penned up along the Atlantic coast. It's not too great a stretch to suggest that Algonkin-speaking peoples also used it to disperse (in a pattern quite like the French), while peoples of the other six families stayed within the logic of their north-south alignments.

If language relations are any indication, the pattern, looking at a modern map, is clear. Only in the unusual geographical circumstance of the Algonkin did people tend from right to left in their broad movements. Instead, over and over, it was up and down along the continent's eastern, middle and western geographical components.

The North American West is full of details of this patterning. The Navajo call themselves Dine (The People), the same term (with the same meaning) that's the tribal designation of Athapaskan speakers more than sixteen hundred miles north in the Canadian West. Uto-Aztecan speakers include Shoshone of the northern Rockies and Great Basin, the Comanche, who migrated southward through the Rockies and onto the southern plains, and far to the south the Aztec, who entered Mexico's central valley from the north in the thirteenth century. After migrating southward onto the plains, the Comanche acquired horses, traded northward to the Missouri River, and raided farther south to the Texas coast and deep into Mexico. The Anasazi of the Southwest were connected to central Mexico by cultural influence and by ties of trade that included jungle parrots. While continental trade certainly moved from coast to coast, the primary routes in the West were along the mountain chains and up and down the Pacific coast and the plains. The Old North Trail was used until recently for journeys from the Canadian plains southward along the Rockies to New Mexico; arguably it's the oldest road in the western hemisphere, following roughly the suggested route of first arrivals through the ice-free corridor out of Alaska.

It's hardly a surprise to find cultural and economic continuities along the same geographical lines. Standard anthropological texts group native peoples into regions according to similar lifeways and means of living: eastern woodlands, plains, southwestern desert, montane, Great Basin, Pacific Northwest. These groupings simply give a name and a shape to what is apparent; namely that peoples living in the same physical setting will find the same ways to feed themselves, and as they move and trade within that same setting their cultures will evolve in similar directions and find similar forms. Because those settings run up and down North America, so do the cultural and economic affinities. Indian peoples of Saskatchewan had more in common with those in the Dakotas, and people in British Columbia with those in Washington and Oregon, than either had with peoples in Ohio or Quebec. The Apache, Pima, and Yaquis of Arizona and northern Mexico fought a lot, but the cultural overlap among them was far greater than with the plains Arapahoe or the Modoc in northern California.

Making points like these quickly becomes an exercise in the obvious. But as I hope my students learn from their experiment with the map of North America, sometimes the obvious is what we tend to overlook. The point here concerns the long history before states were established. Human history of North America is at least twelve thousand years old. The most apparent evidence from the first 11,500 of those years says that when people arranged themselves – when they thought in terms of natural connections to a world beyond their own – they did so along geographical continuities running north and south through the continent. Probably they thought of their broader identities, their associations, and affinities, along those up-and-down lines. It was along those lines that life flowed most normally.

One could travel a long way north and south, along the Pacific coast from Vancouver Island to Baja California or through the Rocky Mountains from Alberta to New Mexico or from the southern plains deep into Canada, and still find people living in roughly similar ways. It would take a far shorter trip east and west, by contrast, for a traveller to find himself in increasingly alien physical and cultural terrain. For the great stretch of time from the first human presence until European arrival, the assumed axis of things must have seemed up and down.

But that axis was about to shift.

* * *

The clearest lesson of this ancient north-south alignment is the astonishing power of state-making. Canada and the United States were created in opposition to the lay of the land and to the flow of events and culture that presumably had dominated life and thinking in North America from its earliest history. People made those two nations by bulling their way crosswise over thousands of years of cultural patterning and historical momentum. Once we truly look at the physical map of North America, the more familiar political map appears stunning. Boundaries that we take for granted today suddenly look arbitrary in the extreme, as if some doodler with a straightedge and a penchant for right angles has randomly sliced up the continent. Most arbitrary of all is the U.S.-Canadian boundary, surely one of the longest nonsensical borders on the planet. From the Lake of the Woods to the Juan de Fuca Straits, the forty-ninth parallel is a fifteen-hundred-mile monument to how political can trump geography.

The creation of North American nations has no competition as the most important development in the last five hundred years of continental history. For the study of the Canadian and the American Wests, this requires of us a deep respect – grudging or wholehearted, depending on our opinions on the outcome – for the forces behind that creation; three in particular. First, a market-driven capitalist economy sent the earliest agents, fur traders, and explorers, to chart the way across the north-south barriers and to begin the inventory of resources. Capitalism's hunger to commodify and develop those resources – the soil and its products, timber and pasture, metals precious and nonprecious, fish and otters and whales – gave a focus and purpose to the seizure of the vast North American West on both sides of the forty-ninth parallel. From the capitalist perspective, in fact, the stark differences among plains and mountains and coast were not a discouragement but an incentive to combine and consolidate those north-south topographical bands. In geography, difference implies variety of resources, and when all resources are potential commodities, that means opportunities are multiplied. In a market economy it makes sense, not to stay within geographical lines, but to cut across them.

A second force, both facilitating and feeding that shared U.S. and Canadian economic drive, was a technological revolution. Resources in western Canada and the United States – copper, timber, coal, and iron – were so desirable because dozens of industrial innovations gave them new uses and meanings. Grabbing those resources now was possible because of even more vigorous innovations in transportation and communication. More improvements were made in the technology of moving people, goods, and information during the nineteenth century than in the twenty centuries before it.

The third force was the governmental apparatus of the states themselves. The central direction of Canada and the United States provided the over-arching authority and political structure to accomplish their coast-to-coast, across-the-grain incorporations of the West's diverse landforms and peoples.

After recognizing the oldest fact in North American history – that what we call the Canadian and U.S. Wests are diverse within themselves and yet bound together geographically, with plains and mountains and coastal continuities running north and south across more than thirty latitudes – there is also this second fact, newer but equally obvious. Western Canada and the western United States also have in common their independent consolidations along lines from east to west, a geographically anomalous alignment born of forces that, more than any others, have shaped the modern world: an international capitalist economy, a technological revolution, and the embrace of localities within increasingly powerful nation states. Like geography, these forces if anything are more pronounced in the West than elsewhere. The resource-rich West inspired the heartiest response of outside capital: fur and railway companies, mining and ranching corporations, shipping firms and mercantile operations. Both Wests have been showplaces of the technological wonders of production, transportation, and communication; silver and gold and copper mines thousands of feet deep, telegraph wires strung to the horizon, the long reach of transcontinental rails, and the mechanical giants of plains agriculture all are properly part of the regions' images. As for the U.S. and Canadian governments, their hands have been much busier out West than back East, starting simply with ownership of land and extending through relations with native peoples, the subsidizing of enterprise and transportation, promoting and maintaining tourism, and many other areas.

Are any themes of continental history more obvious than these two? One dominated the North American story for millennia, the other came late but came on strong. Both are impressive exactly because they are so foundational to our understanding that we are tempted to disregard them. Disregarding them can be a healthy response, much like ignoring water when studying details in the habits of fish. But when looking for basics, in this case the fundamentals of understanding the Canadian and American Wests, sometimes the obvious is exactly where to start.

When we recognize each theme and move them to the front of our attention, they suggest a structure for the study of the North American West. We can picture it as the intersection of influences and historical trends. One set of influences and traditions follows the ancient axis of north and south. We might call them the great meridians, or maybe the tenacious verticals, or the irrepressible longitudes. These influences are rooted in geography and deep history. Overrun in some ways by the making of two nations, they nonetheless persist. Often they exert themselves energetically. The other forces run along the more recent (but now centuries-old) axis of east and west. These we might call the great parallels, or the triumphant horizontals, or the muscular latitudes. These are the influences that swept across the continent to create the political map we take for granted. They continue, often more vigorous than when they plowed their way to the Pacific.

These influences, North America's historical verticals and horizontals, its cultural longitudes and latitudes, naturally are often in conflict, but rarely if ever does one really win. Rather, they continually act upon each other. They mitigate each other's effects. The result is a continuous blend of countervailing dispositions expressed again and again in the Canadian and U.S. Wests in everything from government policies to art and daily habits of language and dress. Just to complicate matters more, there are important differences within the east–west and north–south continuities. Canada and the United States may have been born out of the same impulses to conquer and consolidate the continent, but each nation had its own distinctive story with its own historical wrinkles. Those differences had their effects too. And if Greater Montana and Middle Earth are strikingly distinct from each other, they also vary within themselves. Winter in Saskatchewan differs from winter on the Texas plains; life in Jasper is not the same as life in Santa Fe.

At the risk of pseudo social science, we might approach particular pieces of western history and life by siting them on this grid of influences. We might ask in each case about the relative roles of the westerly drive of state-making and the insistent inclinations of geography and cultural roots, looking also for differences inside these two broad patterns. There is nothing precise in this. To the contrary, anything studied is the result of all the contingencies and the chance turns that make history infinitely variable and utterly unpredictable. What this approach can do, however, is give us a means to organize our thinking about the largest outlines of western North American history as well as the uncountable details that make it up. Similarly to situating a given place cartographically by latitude and longitude and gradations within each, we can roughly locate our Wests and their marvellously diverse particulars at the intersections of influences criss-crossing the continent.

* * *

A few examples can give some body to these abstractions. Take, for instance, native peoples and the question of native identity. An essential part of state-making is the government's power to catalogue and name its constituent parts and to set standards for citizenship. Partly this involves the government's deciding for itself who is in and who is out, politically speaking, but partly it is a matter of convincing various groups that their identities (and presumably allegiances) are with the state being built around it. This job can be more difficult with indigenous peoples than with immigrants. By choosing to leave someplace else, immigrants imply a willingness to live under new rules and to shift their sense of who they are. Not so with indigenous peoples. For many of them membership in the new polity was, to put it mildly, not their preference, and more to the point the notions of a state, its structure and its authority were utterly alien. Their identities instead were usually highly localized in family, band, and tribe, and any wider allegiance usually was with groups within those north-south cultural stripings that ran across, not with, national boundaries. A Blackfoot would likely think of himself as part of a familial lineage and within one of the group's three tribes (Pigeon, Blood, and *Siksika* or Blackfoot proper) with ties to the others and to related tribes like the Gros Ventre, all of which ranged across the forty-ninth parallel and state and provincial boundaries of Montana, Alberta, and Saskatchewan. This clash of patterns was repeated over and over. Official relations with Indians can be read in part as a continuous bouncing around within its contradictions.

It is commonly supposed that Canadian Indian policy has been friendlier and more sensitive than that in the United States. Maybe so in the particulars, but in broadest outlines the two seem much more alike than otherwise. Both grew from the same assumptions – that their nations would include many peoples, that those peoples would hold somewhat to older identities, but that those identities would be subsumed under a collective attachment to a nation and to certain common authorities. Both the United States and Canada recognized degrees of native autonomy, but (the point is so obvious that it is easily overlooked) that autonomy was prescribed – was in effect created – as a national option. John Marshall's famous phrase defining the Cherokees' position exactly caught this tension and its incongruities. While the United States had negotiated with the Cherokee as if they and other tribes were sovereign states like France or England, Marshall wrote, that was a fiction. They were "domestic dependent nations." Each was a nation that existed within another national framework, and so each was domestic, and each was also dependent, since ultimately its safety relied upon that encompassing nation. Paradoxically, a tribe's independence was dependent. Both U.S. and Canadian policies, for all their differences, worked within this same frame. On the one hand they recognized native allegiances and autonomy; on the other they insisted that somehow that autonomy could be lived out inside an authority that made its own rules and set its own limits.

Especially after the Civil War the U.S. government quickly tightened its authority and restricted the tribes, especially in outward expressions of power and visible governing institutions. Agents could remove and replace balky tribal leaders. Serious crimes committed on reservations by Indians against whites already fell under white jurisdiction, but when the Supreme Court ruled in 1883 that only Indians could try an Indian for the murder of one of their own, Congress passed the Major Crimes Act (1885), which placed serious crimes between Indian peoples under the laws of the state or territory surrounding the reservation. In 1871 Washington ended the last vestige of

Indian sovereignty in negotiations by simply declaring that from then on all arrangements would be made, not through treaties, but through congressional action and administrative rulings. Cultural life soon felt the same intensifying assault. The Courts of Indian Offenses, with Indian judges appointed by the government, had authority to prosecute persons practising polygamy and many religious rituals (called "heathenish rites"). Extensive school systems, attendance mandatory and in some cases enforced through seizure of children, had as part of its purpose eradication of native languages, dress, religion, and cultural identity.

The most obvious tact of fitting indigenous peoples into consolidating states was for governments to designate which tribes were legitimate and to define citizenship by drawing lines between who was and was not an Indian. Both governments assumed these powers, with results both troubling and comic. Historians are paying increasing attention to the theme of ethnogenesis: the birth of tribal communities out of the grind and friction of Indian-white relations. Whites tended to assume native peoples were organized politically and socially roughly along the lines of their own states, with centralized leadership and strong common identities among varied components. Typically that was not the case, but in the face of intensifying pressure from white expansion and losses from epidemics on the one hand and, on the other, new opportunities of trade and of conquering other native groups, consolidation into larger entities made increasing sense. Indian "nations," at first a term used by Europeans projecting their own notions of political order on people organized very differently, became more and more an accurate description. In time, tribes began to think even more inclusively in terms of an "Indianess" among tribes, again largely in response to the presence of overwhelming state power. The intrusion of the state, that is, indirectly precipitated basic changes in how native peoples thought of themselves.

Part of this process, of course, involved the state's imposition of categories on native communities. Bands that recognized nothing more than a general kinship among themselves were told that they were now a single people with the same spokesmen for all – usually those leaders willing to treat with white authorities. More problematical were government standards to identify Indians as a racial group, regardless of tribe. The basis typically was family lineage, generally speaking something close to a universal measure to be sure, but native genealogical traditions varied hugely, and any one application of bloodlines inevitably violated dozens of them. Canada's well-known system recognized as Indian the children of an Indian father and white wife, but not an Indian mother with a white husband. The system caused considerable mischief, although it was designed as a protection from white landgrabbers – a danger well illustrated in the United States, where Indians without such a protection suffered massive losses to whites who married their way to tribal property. In both countries, however, being an Indian increasingly was a matter of following cultural norms. Here the state's imposition went beyond a relatively objective system of lineage to sets of values and behaviours. Indians became whites if they acted like whites; white behaviour being defined as conforming to institutions and values being laid down from the Atlantic toward the Pacific. The United States codified this notion in the Dawes Severalty Act (1887), Canada in the Indian Act (1876), which built upon the Enfranchisement Act (1869) and the revealingly named Gradual Civilization Act (1857).

Indian peoples, on the other hand, have shown some facility in working to their indigenous advantage these impositions of the state, starting with the border itself. Most famously in the cases of the Lakota Sioux under Sitting Bull and some Nez Percé remnants after Chief Joseph's surrender, groups in the United States used the artificial boundary of the forty-ninth parallel to find temporary sanctuary from efforts to confine them to reservations. On the Canadian side, Métis and their leader Louis Riel found refuge to the south.

As for government efforts to define tribal identities and to structure and control native authority, no one has to look far to notice the limits of that effort. One of the most undertold stories in both U.S. and Canadian history is how native leaders have manoeuvred within state authority to preserve cultural integrity. One tack has been to mitigate and compromise official controls, another has been the persistence of traditional authorities; in effect shadow systems that are localized and rooted in varied customs of status, prestige, and consensus. Also persisting are tribal divisions and feuds, some arising from rival responses within tribes to the white challenge but many from purely internal disputes and contentious memories. Religious practices survive, some of them syncretic evolutions borrowing from Christianity. The closer one examines native communities in the West, the more one appreciates the survival of outward traditions and inward identities, and the harder one looks at those survivals, the subtler they seem in their variations. The juggernaut of state power outwardly dominates, but the mosaic of peoples and cultures remains fundamental to the North American West.

Indians have been the people most vulnerable in the process of state making, and they have had the most to lose. Consequently their stories are among the most troubling and heroic. One such story – that of the Cree – is set along the boundary between Canada and the United States. The Cree were one of many peoples drawn more deeply onto the plains by adopting the horse and hunting the bison. By the 1880s they faced a familiar crisis with the shrinkage of the bison herds and a growing pressure from the Canadian government to curtail their movements in return for rations. A portion of the tribe under Little Bear chose to move to Montana. This, however, left them in national limbo. U.S. authorities called them Canadian, but the Canadians said that since the Cree had signed a treaty, and because Little Bear's followers had not signed, they must not be Cree. To twist John Marshall's phrase, they were domestic *independent* people, and with their home now split between two nations, each insisting that everyone fit the identity of one or the other, that was about as bad a position as was possible to be in. In effect they were nobody. During one brutal winter, the Cree survived on the frozen carcasses of coyotes poisoned by ranchers. Soldiers harassed them for years. In 1896 Lt. John J. (later "Black Jack") Pershing rounded up most of them and expelled them to Canada, but most soon returned. Twenty years later the U.S. Congress created the Rocky Boy reservation and these Cree finally accepted a niche with the new national order.

* * *

This same patterning appears in the daily lives of those who came West and of their descendants. Once we look for it, we can see it in familiar icons of the westering experience. What was a sod hut, after all, but a concession by immigrants to the demands and limits of the plains? And although not recognized at the time, it was in mimic of a style found up and down the meridians of Middle Earth; the Pawnee and other peoples lived along streams (also the strong preference of homesteaders) and built earth lodges often bermed in the style of settler's dugouts. But go inside these similar shelters and you will see starkly different cultural worlds. A Pawnee earth lodge would show the familial arrangement, weaponry, and tools established for generations among plains natives, and if the dwelling was that of a holy man its alignment with points of the compass and with the solstices as well as the articles around its altar would suggest religious traditions common among plains peoples. A soddie's interior, on the other hand, was an intense material expression of values being carried east to west. Its details were the agonized choices by families moving from Ohio or Ontario to Nebraska or Saskatchewan, the distilled essence of what they thought most representative of their mother cultures – books, fragile dishes, family clocks, treasured furniture, lace tablecloths, and their own religious basics, Bibles and crosses. When itinerant photographers stopped by to record families who had achieved some stability and success, parents and children dressed in their best and hauled their proudest treasures out to pose with them: fine tables, easy chairs, pump organs.

Every region of pioneer settlement can be sited at the same sort of cultural coordinates. The first ranchers on the plains and in the Great Basin set up operations along the very streams where Indian peoples had set their winter camps, and did so for the same reasons. Geography required that anyone hoping to survive the winters and to raise domestic animals, whether horses or cattle, had to stick to the streambeds with their sheltering trees and swards of forage. Move westward across enough meridians, settlers found new elemental facts of life made adaptations unavoidable, and the most obvious ones resembled arrangements used by Indians for centuries. Ironically, the newcomers' deference to this traditional Indian way of life brought immediate trouble. The fundamental cause of the conflict between Euro-Americans and Native Americans was the fact that, quite literally, they found common ground; both peoples had to obey the same environmental rules, which meant both had to hold onto the same limited ecological spaces, which meant one side had to give way or both had to fight.

But if whites and Indians fought because both had to conform to the realities of meridians, the struggle itself displayed the terrible strength of forces that ran along the parallels. Even as they adapted to the new environment, the east-to-west invaders brought the focused power of the numbers, the technology, the economic drive, and the centralized command of a consolidating modern state. With so much behind them, drawing on enormous imported resources, the victorious newcomers then could try to defy the most hallowed geographical imperatives. Within their arbitrary political boundaries the U.S. and Canadian governments divided land by equally imperious systems, most notably in the vast checkerboard grid of the U.S. land survey, lines oblivious to the watersheds and landforms that had dictated human arrangements for thousands of years. Both the United States and Canada went farther, determined to transform into farms the land that lay outside and above the valleys watered and silted by streams – the huge expanse of grasslands, 95 percent of the plains – that always had been the domain of grazers. Subsidized by official policy and by the capital and technology of railroads, hopeful farmers busted the sod; smitten by the dream of supplying distant markets, they planted crops on millions of acres that had never known cultivation.

The same sets of realities – the persistence of the verticals and the imposition of the horizontals – played out in numberless towns sprouting across the interior Canadian and American Wests. Like farms and ranches, they typically were located along streams and were required in many ways to cope with the dwarfing landscape where they had been plopped down. More often than not each was also an eastern grid of streets stamped generically onto the land, and along them sprang up frame houses of styles and furnishings from the East as well as public buildings housing institutional transplants – churches, fraternal lodges, banks. Many of these streets were named Elm, Chestnut, Walnut, and Oak in recognition of the saplings planted at their edges for future shade and cultural resonance, carried into plains and deserts along parallels from the forested East.

This same tension – the push of culture westward and its translation into western geographies – expressed itself most intimately within families that settled in western Canada and the United States. Out of these households came breathing, walking artifacts of the process that made the Canadian and American Wests – the children. Parents concerned about transplanting their traditions and values into the new country saw in their sons and daughters the ultimate tests of success. They taught them songs and invoked family stories to teach various lessons. They read to them from sacred religious texts, literary classics, and popular works shot through with moral truisms. When possible they kept the family joined to its distant roots through another governmental connector: the postal systems. (Late in the pioneering era, the mails became giant conduits of transplanted material life; catalogues of Sears, Roebuck and Company and Montgomery Ward were perhaps the most efficient conveyors of culture in history up to that time.) Quickly settlers established schools, often pooling their own money before state support was available. Their concern was to educate the young not only in the three R's and other basics, but also in broader cultural allegiances, especially the one that overlay everything else in the march of the horizontals across the continent: patriotism, identity with the state.

The efforts paid off. Every western child of that first generation was to some degree an imprint of the culture being brought into the country. Yet every girl and boy inevitably grew into adulthood shaped as well by the country itself. She or he likely spent thousands of hours working independently outdoors, under parents' orders but beyond their influence. A child learned much about who he or she was by testing abilities in a world fundamentally different from the previous generation's. Most of all, children absorbed the uncountable messages of their surroundings that together defined for them what was normal, established likes and dislikes, and forged between themselves and their environment attachments at least as powerful as those with their parents and their parents' heritages.

Children of the Canadian and U.S. Wests had in common this mixed legacy. Growing up on one side of the border or the other made some difference, of course; Canadian institutions and attitudes were not those of the United States, and neither were their effects on the rising generation. Differences, however, developed within a binding similarity. A blending of imported influences with the dispositions of particular western places together shaped young westerners of both nations and set them both apart from cousins in the East. On this point we have plenty of testimony from the children themselves. A broad theme running through their reminiscences is of the lessons taught and traditions instilled by those who brought them west and how those influences were all wound together with their own identification with their birth land, its people and history, and its sensual particulars.

Like the story of the Cree, one of the most eloquent of these memoirs is set along the national boundary. Wallace Stegner's *Wolf Willow* is his account of returning as a man to his boyhood home near Eastend, Saskatchewan. His memories there feel superficial until the scent of wolf willows by the Whitemud (aka Frenchman) River instantly takes him back, fully and viscerally. It is a primal memory, part of that grooving of the brain that happens only in childhood and seals an emerging identity with a particular place. Stegner's encounter with the smell of willow is a fitting start to a reminiscence and regional history that can be read, among many ways, as a cross-hatching of what shaped the distinctive plains society of his youth. He tells of his father's obsessive drive to change the country and make it pay, a microcosm of a society's determination, and he recalls the overbearing weather and climate that continuously blunted that drive. The entire narrative is a similar mix: Mounties, boyhood experiences as vivid as willow-sniffing, fur traders and their native allies and wives, the railroad, and the Métis, themselves an intersection of the east-to-west push and the Indians and Indian ways always part of the cultural landscape. In the story of Eastend, this great writer of the Canadian and U.S. Wests is telling us of a region's collective inheritance that in turn was embodied in every child who grew up within it. "The years during which I participated in the birth of that town were the shaping years of my life," he wrote elsewhere: "I have never forgotten a detail of them."

* * *

Some final examples can be drawn from one of the most vital areas of life in the contemporary West: tourism. The east-to-west impulse at its most powerful was developmental, dedicated to wringing wealth from the land and making it work on the terms that were brought to it, acted out by invasive corporations and by men like Stegner's father, ever on the hunt for the Big Rock Candy Mountain. But almost from the start there was a second impulse. This eastern desire was to experience first-hand the West's magnificent geography. Its inspiration was the universal appeal of beautiful country and the romantic impulse to escape the very way of life settlers were trying to implant out West – the developed world of towns and cities and institutions.

Here was cultural cross-hatching at its subtlest, and to some of us, its most intriguing. The desire itself was one of those projections out of Europe and the Atlantic coast across the interior to the Pacific. Yet the thing desired – what was being imposed onto the West – was the insistence that the West *not* change, that it retain what outsiders considered its distinctiveness. Unlike the drives to force native identities into the state's categories, to make the landscape conform to other means of production, and to graft into the West other traditions, this one relied on the West's differences.

What attracted outsiders was the jarring dissonance they felt when they brought their perceptions of normal geography and biota and their expectations of customary culture into the new country. Basically, the lure was in how east-to-west perceptions clashed with the West's north-to-south realities.

Basically, but not exactly. Considerable stretches of the West had little appeal to eastern escapist sensibilities – the lava beds of Idaho, much of the Great Basin, a good portion of the Canadian and U.S. grasslands, eastern Oregon's marshes, and the remoter regions of the Canadian Rockies. Outlanders, furthermore, wanted western landscapes to conform to what they thought they were, or ought to be. Culturally, they were interested in particular aspects of western life – certain native cultures (but not others) and what passed as the most colourful phases of the pioneering experience. Urban life in places like Denver or Seattle did not qualify. What was sought was the West of Imagination, a perceived unchanging landscape, a geographical fly in amber that was, furthermore, cleansed of any unsightliness from an earlier era. Cattle and mining towns have been favourites, always with a Boot Hill but never with cholera. As for visits to "the wild," tourists' contact was increasingly choreographed and the sights were dressed to meet expectations of the growing number of constituents. Eventually the U.S. National Park Service employed hundreds of landscape architects. This West, whether the wilderness or the frontier of cowtowns and Indian villages, also was expected to be accessible and graced with at least minimal amenities. Parks like Yellowstone, portrayed as the wild antithesis of modern developed communities, in fact became some of the region's most commercialized real estate.

Tourist destinations that drew their appeal from wild geography and cultural set pieces, in short, ought to be seen as the Canadian and American West's persisting, but on terms of the East. The results have been some of the continent's best illustrations of an increasingly common paradox of modern life. They are representations of themselves.

But as with those determined efforts to transform the West in its human identities, its means of production and working landscapes, and its traditions, this drive met resistance from enduring cultural and geographical conditions.

The West will take its own shape, regardless of efforts to keep it the same or to fashion it into its idealized self. The biota of national parks continually evolves, frequently in unpredictable directions. Visitors marvel at herds of elk as proof of a park's pristine character. In fact the decline of their predators has produced a boom of the antlered population, which has led to overgrazing of willows and young aspens, which has increased erosion and helped dry up wetlands, which, with the loss of trees for their lodges, severely threatens communities of beavers. (In a lovely irony, beavers have prospered in subdivisions where homeowners plant plenty of trees to give their yards the look of a natural landscape.) The elk-beaver relationship is an allegory of the ultimately irresistible dynamism of the West as a living environment – something that might be said as well about cultural life that persists within the West of tourism. The creation of virtually every national park in both nations involved the expulsion of native peoples whose ancestors had used those places well for generations. Having Indians actually *in* the parks would puncture the illusion of an utterly natural landscape, so they had to go. Recently, however, governments are beginning to bring the long human story into their interpretations, sometimes taking the radical step of bringing native peoples actively into park management.

Consequently, tourist sites, accessible and aggressively publicized, are among the clearest demonstrations of the continuous interplay of eastern insistence and western persistence. Economically strapped cattlemen hold onto the essentials of a way of life by supplementing ranching by hosting "city slicker" vacationers, who spend days in the saddle and sleep on the ground during semi-fantasized cattle drives. Indian powwows are remarkable amalgams of tradition and innovation, tribal and pan-tribal identities, all acted out through dress, chants, dances, food, and folk art. In towns like Jasper and Jackson Hole tourists flirt with the wilderness West. Surrounded by spectacular vistas, pilgrims browse shops with names like The Grinning Grizzly to buy shirts made in the Philippines and emblazoned with wilderness logos. Next they might strike off on trails through terrain of genuinely enduring topology and wild animal communities. A few hikers will be mauled or die from falls or succumb to hypothermia during sudden storms. The vast majority will return, perhaps ending the day in self-consciously rough-hewn eateries sipping local microbrews and dining on bison and trout (some imported frozen from

Japan). Most will go home satisfied they have moved from their own world into quite another by following a horizontal across North America's indelible vertical striping.

In some western places this interplay is nicely condensed and showcased. Lake Louise in Alberta's Banff National Park offers unmatched views of what outsiders consider the essential Canadian Rockies – a glacier-fed lake in a glacier-gouged valley, a place of its own beauty yet resonating with Europe's favourite alpine scenery, as implied in the magnificent chateau-style hotel on the shore. Advertised as remote from the busy world (a "diamond in the wilderness"), Lake Louise was first promoted by the most potent force in drawing the West into the East's embrace, the Canadian Pacific Railroad. This phenomenon – the great east-to-west unifier, selling the West as forever distinct and separate – has had several parallels in the United States, most notably in the Great Northern Railroad's marketing vacations to Glacier National Park, and the Atchison, Topeka and Santa Fe creating the image of an exotic, ever-different Southwest of the Grand Canyon and changeless Indian peoples. Not far southeast of Lake Louise is Calgary, another railroad creation, flooded each July by crowds drawn to the Calgary Stampede. This civic fest began as an agricultural exhibition, a show of pride in the transformation of plains into garden that was so much a part of modern state-making. It evolved, however, into a celebration of cowboy culture, which in turn is both a distinct working tradition uniting the Canadian and U.S. plains from the Gulf coast to northern Alberta and an outlander's paramount vision of a West forever apart. The Stampede's centrepiece is a world-class rodeo, but just as alluring are the attendant attractions of walking the streets in western duds and spilling beer with actual cowboys in saloons with names like Outlaws and the Golden Garter.

* * *

Tourists are right. The Canadian and U.S. Wests are different from the Canadian and U.S. Easts, although the differences are subtler, and their historical roots more complicated, than most of us appreciate. Nearly four centuries ago John Smith reminded us of the need to bring geography to our history and narrative to our geography. Nowhere is his call more pertinent than in the study of the western reaches of the United States and Canada.

Geography's imprint on history there is indelible, and especially since John Smith's day history has flexed its power over the land to a truly extraordinary degree. To borrow Smith's terms, our challenge is to enliven the carcass of an unpeopled map and to ensure all vagrant stories are settled in their proper homes. Each task is necessarily in tension with the other, but it's an especially creative tension and so is all to the good.

NOTE

1   Editors' note: Throughout this work, we have allowed authors to choose the protocol for the use of Blackfoot versus Blackfeet. There are at least three variations of which we are aware: Canadian versus United States designations, tribal versus individual identifications, and Confederacy versus individual tribe. Each author chose the variation that best suits his or her purposes.

Two Faces West: The Development Myth in Canada and the United States

Donald Worster, University of Kansas

A locomotive whistles shrilly as it approaches a small town on the North American prairie. Along the tracks ahead stands a grain elevator on one side, a wooden station and a brick hotel on the other, behind them a checkerboard of streets marking off a community's life. On the outskirts of the town a woman peers from her farmhouse window, watching the train approach against a background of snow-crusted mountains. A man ploughing a field, preparing to plant wheat, stops to watch and listen too. All these images have been popular in the Canadian and American West for more than a century. They are signs of what the two nations have in common – a landscape, a technology, a set of hopes, a story of development.

These two nations share other signs and memories as powerful as that prairie scene, including the sound of a beaver slapping its tail on a lake; the sight of bison streaming over a wide plain, and of their carcasses lying in the grass; of cattle bawling and shoving in, taking the bison's place; of oil wells pumping wealth from the ground, smelly and viscous; of gold dust glinting in the bottom of a miner's pan, mixed with gravel and snow melt. Both nations have displaced proud Indian peoples who once occupied the land and are now living on the margins, expected to turn to farming or manufacturing to survive.

Both nations have witnessed a diverse immigration of Chinese railroad workers, Russian peasant farmers, French or Spanish missionaries in black robes, and millions of English-speaking poor people.

Despite all these commonalities, however, interesting differences have separated the Canadian from the American West. There have been differences, for example, in the Indian policies followed on either side of the border and in the degree of violence that has occurred between native inhabitants and white Europeans. Historians have compared the "Wild West" of America to the "Mild West" of Canada.[1] Rather than treading down that familiar path, I want to suggest another comparison between our two countries, and between the two Wests within them, by focusing on a seemingly more innocuous subject, the idea of development. Despite its prosaic if not trite sound, that idea offers a fresh, provocative basis for exploring our differences. Canadian historians, like their American counterparts, have frequently told the story of the West as a story of development, writing extensively on the development of railroads, industry, agriculture, towns and cities, culture, religion, and universities. That fact may not seem very noteworthy, but I want to argue that it is highly significant. Ubiquity, familiarity, and habit have all made us indifferent toward what we have been saying or about how we have imagined the past. There has been too little critical inquiry on either side of the Canadian-U.S. border into what the word development has meant, into its darker implications, including the costs of development both for people and nature, or into the question of how well the development idea accounts for our distinctive national and regional characteristics.

Both Canadians and Americans have given one fundamental meaning to development from which all other meanings derive: development refers to exploiting the land to get the wealth out of it. "Undeveloped" land is land that lacks roads, buildings, or mines; it is land that produces little or no profit. There is very little difference between the two nations in this regard. When the two Wests were at an early stage in that exploitation, they both saw themselves as economically underdeveloped, or put more positively, as economically developing – the advancing edge of the world's first new nations. Today, on the other hand, both Wests see themselves as having mature, well-financed, and well-developed economies, though both also describe themselves as still developing in the sense that all regions and nations see themselves as tirelessly driving to turn nature into wealth, with no end in sight.

Even on this basic level of economics, however, the word development has had a complicated set of meanings. Development first came into common use in the nineteenth century, an era that was awestruck by advances in biological science that had begun to show how organisms mature and evolve, not only growing in size but changing in form, passing from youth to maturity or from the one-celled amoeba to the multi-celled plant or animal. By analogy, human social development was supposed to follow a similar progression of stages, as natural as the passage from the embryo to the adult, starting with the savage life and ending up with the English gentleman. This idea of development as the progressive law of nature inspired not only the Victorians, but also such social philosophers as Karl Marx and Friedrich Engels, for whom history was an inexorable advance from primitive society to industrial capitalism and on to a socialist future, all stages in the technological domination of nature. According to Gustavo Esteva, "development became the central category of Marx's work: revealed as a historical process that unfolds with the same necessary character of natural laws."[2]

In the nineteenth century, development also became a transitive verb, with humans as the subject, nature as the object. That is, it became man's proper role on earth to "develop nature," meaning to make nature over into useful, marketable commodities. Undomesticated nature, civilized people believed, was incomplete and embryonic, a possibility waiting to be achieved. The special role of humankind was to release nature from its slumber, awaken its potentialities, and enable it to reach its grand destiny, which was nothing less than service to our own species' comfort and well-being. This second use of the word as a transitive verb first became popular in the outposts of the British Empire, particularly Australia and Canada, and later in the United States. The Australian scholar H. W. Arndt, who has written an interesting history of the word, quotes an 1846 article in the Canadian Economist: "Canada is now thrown upon her own resources, and if she wishes to prosper, these resources must be developed."[3] Challenged to achieve a measure of independence, Canadians understood that they must become an active agency in nature, no longer content to buy many of their necessities from England.

Development thus became a compelling international myth about the growth of nation-states. By myth I mean simply that it told a popular story about origins and destiny, one progressing from primitive life to civilization, from the simple to the complex, from an inferior colonial dependency to nation-state maturity – a heroic story that both capitalists and communists could share because it expressed their common ideals. The myth was part of the justification of European imperialism – helping other peoples achieve their own state-based identities and secure places in the global economy. It told what all people's attitudes and behaviour toward the rest of nature ought to be, especially among those backward areas far from the centres of civilization. By the time of World War II the myth of development had spread everywhere, replacing older traditions of stasis and equilibrium, and wherever it went it offered a similar formula for improving the life of the nation and its people, one measured in higher per capita income and, so the promise goes, greater happiness and moral enlightenment.[4]

Because the United States and Canada emerged as nations during the very era when development was becoming the dominant political myth, their national histories were both conceived in terms of the myth. However, not one but two stories emerged to describe North American national development. Historians have analyzed them in isolation from one another, but I want to consider them together as different versions of the same myth. Both predict the final success of industrial capitalism, but then they veer off into different emphases and implications; and those differences reveal a great deal about each nation, especially how each has envisioned its place in history and how each has conceived of its relation with nature in the New World. We should not exaggerate the differences, for there are common elements, nor should we minimize their continuing power and persistence in the writing of history.

The first of those two stories may be summed up in these famous words: "The existence of an area of free land, its continuous recession, and the advance of American settlement westward, explain American development."[5] They come, of course, from Frederick Jackson Turner, whose frontier thesis, first presented in 1893, spawned an influential American school of development thinking. Turner was mainly interested in the origins of liberal democracy, which was an American invention in his view, and he saw it deriving from the extraordinary potential of the American land – its untapped abundance.

True to his age, Turner portrayed nature as undeveloped raw material inviting a series of resource exploiters, beginning with traders and trappers, followed by ranchers, miners, and farmers, a succession of single individuals who gave way eventually to a more impersonal set of exploiting institutions in the form of cities, factories, corporations, and the nation-state. Turner accepted this growing exploitation of nature, even celebrated it, although ironically at the same time he celebrated the American love affair with a glorious pristine wilderness.

The most distinctive theme in Turner's story is the notion that development in America is always starting over, like an organism that returns repeatedly to its embryonic state. "All peoples show development," Turner acknowledged, but only in America did development become not a single linear process but a whole series of new beginnings, a process of birth and rebirth. "American social development," he pointed out, "has been continually beginning over again on the frontier."[6] Each new frontier offered an exhilarating moment of what we might call "un-development," when complex European civilization reverted to a more archaic life. From that moment came a sense of freedom from distant centres of power, a freedom that spawned democracy, egalitarianism, and individualism. Regrettably, Turner wrote, the rebirthing opportunities eventually must end, and development must become a fixed linear progression here as in Europe, leading to a single common destiny. Turner found that outcome disturbing because increasingly the American scene would become unfriendly to the freedom and democracy that had come out of the primitive wilderness. He could only hope that what had been so often born and reborn would not quickly fade away.[7]

North of the Great Lakes we find quite another story of development appearing. Often referred to as metropolitanism, it was the creation of such famous Canadian historians as Harold Innis, Arthur Lower, and Donald Creighton, writing in the 1920s and 1930s, and more recently of Maurice Careless. All were as fascinated as Turner with the great interior of North America – its forests, grasslands, waterways, and wildlife – and with the dramatic changes in the natural environment following European settlement. However, the Canadians could find none of Turner's multiple new beginnings in the wilderness; instead, they saw development as a straight-forward march, controlled and directed by metropolitan forces far removed from the interior.

The march had begun in Europe, and it was Europe's urban centres that continued to set the pace, along with the rising Canadian centres of Toronto and Montreal. Cities defined what development meant, they made sure that development was secure and orderly, and they propelled the frontier through its various stages of progress, from gathering beaver pelts to planting wheat.[8]

Despite this strikingly different emphasis on continuity with Europe, Canada's historians seem to have been at times as nationalistic and exceptionalist as those in the United States. For them as for Turner, the natural environment played a major role in creating a national identity, giving Canada a peculiar place among the older nations of the world. Their wilderness condition forced Canadians to become harvesters of raw natural resources called staples. "The trade in staples," wrote Harold Innis, "... has been responsible for various peculiar [i.e., distinctive] tendencies in Canadian development." Beaver was one of the most important of those staple products, he argued, and beaver had made a unique nation to the north, while fish, lumber, and wheat would contribute to its further growth.[9] If Canada looked to England for its model of economic progress, it also depended on those staples taken from and determined by nature. To be sure, in Innis's view as in Turner's, European technology must eventually overcome environmental factors, bringing industrial development. "The geographic unity of Canada which resulted from the fur trade," he wrote, "became less noticeable with the introduction of capitalism and the rail-roads."[10] Their effect was to free the country, region by region, from a dependence on the local products of nature while increasing that on technology and distant markets. Nonetheless, Canada's special historical relation with nature in the New World would never altogether lose its significance. The primitive extraction of fur and pine would leave its trace on Canadian identity.

Another leader of the metropolitan school, Donald Creighton, echoed this ambiguity about Canada's relation to the Old World. Following the standard terms of European development, he argued that Canada had emerged as a vibrant "commercial empire" by exploiting the vast St. Lawrence River system.[11] The phrase "commercial empire" indicated that the country was not traditional in its relation with nature; it was modern and capitalistic, with businessmen rather than armies at its centre. Yet those businessmen, Creighton suggested, even while following the established European model, had their lives shaped in subtle ways by the power of nature; the very form of the St. Lawrence waterway, for instance, gave shape to their enterprise.

Like Turner's frontier story, this metropolitan story has had its own rich mythic potential. Canadians have liked to describe themselves as gathering staples from a vast northern country while becoming spiritually part of what they exploit. A nation pursuing capitalistic gain with great fervour, all the while remaining faithful to an ancient cultural heritage. A nation bringing law and order to the continent while obeying the laws of nature. A nation of traditionalists, unlike the Americans, yet like the Americans creating a distinctive civilization from the Europeans. While Turner hoped his countrymen would always remember their wilderness past as they made more and more money, the Canadians hoped that they would remain true to their European heritage while doing the same. Although both myths ended up in exactly the same place – in a powerful industrial-capitalist economy ransacking the land for raw materials – they arrived there with different memories of where they had been, of what nature had allowed them to do, and of what their relation to the Old World had been.

For reasons that Canada's historians understand better than anyone else, Turner's frontierism never quite caught on north of the border, although it has had a few advocates.[12] On the other hand, the metropolitan school of Canadian history has recently begun to creep south and influence a few American scholars. A leading example is William Cronon's recent book *Nature's Metropolis: Chicago and the Great West*, published in 1991, which is clearly indebted to the staples history of Innis, the commercial empire history of Creighton, the forest history of Lower, and the urban history of Maurice Careless.[13] Like his Canadian teachers, Cronon shifts the development focus from the frontier to the city, repudiating Turner's legacy.[14] He puts ambitious capitalists at the centre of the story, men who set out to remake the face of the land, becoming developers on a continental scale, building railroads from Chicago into the prairies while using the Great Lakes as a supplementary mode of transportation. They transform the broad countryside into a mechanized, commercial system of agriculture and forestry, and they bring the land's products into the city for mass consumption.

Cronon's book is an important work not only in the new frontier and western history but also in the field of environmental history, which deals with human relations with nature. Among other things, he is concerned with the impact that urban people have had on nature, with the ecological consequences of their consumption. In keeping with the conventions of development thinking, however, Cronon portrays nature through most of the book as passive before the onslaught of boosters, businessmen, and consumers. Nature provides a flow of commodities, but in that role it is responsive to whatever demands men make, never becoming an active or disruptive obstacle in their way or forcing them to adapt. Nature does not wreak any vengeance, despite the many ravages committed by capital. The urban consumers, for all their ignorance and indifference toward the land that supports them, apparently suffer no disruption when they deplete the land. In the face of capitalism's overwhelming power, nature rapidly disappears from the scene, becoming transformed into what Cronon calls "second nature," an artificial world designed according to "the logic of capital."[15] Like the nineteenth-century's natural law of development, Cronon's logic of capital moves across the landscape like an iron horse of destiny, and so the book suggests, it is irrational and futile to oppose its progress.

Yet despite his fascination with the transforming logic of capital, Cronon also describes, with all the ambivalence of the Canadian metropolitan historians, a permanent legacy of nature for American cultural life. That legacy is a new region we now call the Midwest. The "logic of nature" turns out to be as important as the logic of capital to the making of that region. Corn and hogs coming into the metropolis from Iowa farmlands are the products of ancient prairie soils, while the beef cattle coming in from the grasslands to the west and southwest are the products of lands that are too dry to become a corn belt. The wood that furnishes housing for Chicago's immigrant multitudes is the product of the white pine forests of Michigan and Wisconsin, which have their own value and reason for existing. Depleting or destroying any of these environmental support systems must have a profound impact on the fate of the Midwest. Nature is, therefore, not truly passive before the onslaught of economic development; capital says to nature, here is what we intend to do in this place, and nature replies, here is what you *may* do. So a reader of the book may find in its narrative more than one conclusion. As in the writing of so many of Canada's great metropolitan historians, an ambivalence between admiring the invading, unstoppable power of the metropolis and admiring the absorbing, shaping power of nature lies at the heart of Cronon's book.

Both of these influential schools of North American history, frontierism and metropolitanism, focus on the process of economic and social development. Both define development as man's inexorable conquest over nature, of ever-greater levels of wealth accumulation, of an increasing degree of technological control. Both see the process leading to the triumph of industrial capitalism on a global scale, and both hint of a withering away of national and regional distinctions. Then, unexpectedly, both schools of history reveal in culture and in nature, working together, an alternative to international homogeneity. In contrast to the classical development myth, both testify that people have not wanted exactly the same thing, that Canadians and Americans have wanted different things – different relationships with the wilderness, different relations with Old World culture, different relations with capital. They also suggest that nature does not always give people what they want, that nature has a continuing power over our lives, a power the development myth never allowed for. Thus, according to our historians, environmental differences (soil, climate, vegetation, the flow of waters) as well as cultural differences separate our two nations from each other, as they separate us from the European centres of civilization; and such differences also show up *within* the two nations, creating many distinctive regions, like the prairie West, out of a single continental whole.

Let us now turn to the westernmost part of North America to see how the same international mythology of development has come into this country too, but, here as elsewhere, has had surprising, unpredictable outcomes. Again, the story takes an unanticipated turn or two, despite the spread of those homogenizing railroads and grain elevators and oil wells. By the western regions I mean the Canada that lies beyond the Shield, beginning with Manitoba and going on to British Columbia; and I mean the United States that lies west of the Mississippi Valley, beginning with the Great Plains and stretching on to the Pacific Coast.[16] Neither has developed into a form that any European thinker, or for that matter any early historian from Ontario or Wisconsin, ever quite anticipated. If we take the coming of transcontinental railroads as signalling the beginning of full-fledged capitalist development in these two regions, then we have on the American side of the border the critical date of

1869, the year of the golden spike, and on the Canadian side the year 1885, the year of the plain iron spike – a mere sixteen-year gap. Before those dates there had been a great deal of exploring, trapping, mining, even some farming; but the railroads were to be the magical key that would release the land from its bondage.[17] In 1862 the Americans passed the Homestead Act, and ten years later the Canadians passed the Dominion Lands Act, both of which aimed to give land to family homesteaders. In each country the official plan of development required the enticement of immigrants out of Europe to resettle on New World soil, raising crops to sell to people in eastern cities, and buying finished goods from those cities. Thus, wheat was as critical as railroads. As a further part of the plan, each nation set up protective tariffs for their eastern manufacturers to secure an advantage in selling finished goods to western farmers.

Canadians call this triad of policies – a transcontinental railroad, an immigration and homesteading program, and a protective tariff for manufacturers – the "National Policy" and they credit Prime Minister John A. Macdonald with implementing it, though graciously acknowledging that he borrowed most of it from the United States.[18] It was not truly an American invention any more than it was Canadian; in its broad outlines the plan followed the international logic of capitalist development.[19]

If we look closely at the two development plans, we can detect small but intriguing differences. Canada, for example, was more accommodating to collective settlement, so that closely knit ethnic groups like the Doukhobors could settle here easily.[20] Canada also was more friendly to rancher-capitalists than the United States government initially was. As David Breen has argued. Alberta set up a generous policy of leasing land on a large scale to cattlemen, though within a few decades, as more farmers arrived in the province and as ranchers in the United States got more recognition, the differences became harder to spot.[21] The railroad picture is more complicated in the United States where many private corporations competed against each other and where no government-owned railroad was ever attempted.[22] With such exceptions, the two nations did set off on similar paths to make the western part of the continent over into a land of open opportunity.

Here is how nature thwarted their grand designs. In the western part of the United States, the land proved far too arid to suit the original plans of railroad executives or government officials. Their logic of national development met a rugged desert and its semi-arid fringe, and it began to run off the tracks. Even Turner, with his vision of a continually rejuvenating life in the wilderness, ran off the tracks. Early on, he had written that it would be useful to know how environment played a part in "determining our lines of development," words that would later come back to haunt him.[23] Three years after his essay on the significance of the frontier, Turner discovered the writings of the explorer John Wesley Powell, who described a West that was more arid than anything Turner had ever experienced.[24] Powell was not only the first American to make a comprehensive analysis of those arid conditions in the West (published in 1878), he was also one of the first to envision America as a land of diverse regions shaped by natural conditions. Turner himself, after reading Powell, began looking into the ways in which his abstract "wilderness" was a complicated mosaic of natural environments, with diverse implications for development, though he could never quite figure out how to talk about that unfamiliar country beyond the hundredth meridian.

Other Americans did learn how, but doing so required a major revision in their thinking about development. The most serious weakness lay in the Homestead Act and its ambitious promise of an agricultural empire, a dream coming out of places like Illinois, Ohio, and Virginia, and drawing on older European models. Capital and labour together could not find a way to make that dream real in places like Idaho and Arizona. Both interests were forced to turn to the federal government as the chief organizer and bankroller of agricultural development in the West if they were to go forward. Beginning in 1902 the U.S. government undertook to reclaim arid lands through large irrigation projects. To a degree unprecedented in the East, the West henceforth became the protégé of the federal government, the beneficiary of what now, at modern prices, amounts to several hundred billion dollars' worth of infrastructure investment.

That unanticipated outcome was ironic in the extreme. Compared to Canadians, Americans were not accustomed to looking favourably on a strong, centralized state. Admitting their dependence on that state meant contradicting their self-image of frontier individualism and freedom of enterprise, but the environmental conditions of the West forced them do just that – to adopt radical new policies, to look eastward for water. Consequently, the real American West, the West of fact rather than romance, became the domain of the Bureau of Reclamation and the Bureau of Land Management more than of Wyatt Earp or Billy the Kid.

One might call this outcome a triumph for metropolitanism, since it was the federal capital that henceforth began to lead and control western development. No more than the western frontiersman or the Chicago capitalist, however, was the federal bureaucracy prepared to cope with the western environment. It is still not prepared to do so today. After nearly a century of federally funded water projects, the American West remains highly vulnerable to aridity: on the Great Plains, where another dust bowl disaster is never far off; in the southwestern deserts, which are still deserts the last time anyone looked; and indeed around every western city except those located in the narrow, humid coastal strip of Oregon and Washington. The dream of developing the West into an empire inhabited by millions of agricultural producers has not come true on anything like the scale the dreamers hoped, and even where agriculture has succeeded, as it has in California's Central Valley, it remains extremely vulnerable to the limits of nature and to its own excesses: dams are silting up, soil salinity is increasing, the heavy pesticide use associated with irrigation is meeting public resistance, and there are fiercely competing claims on the limited supply of water. As other countries have discovered, water development is a far more uncertain, destructive, and expensive undertaking than we once thought – any of us, but the metropolitan elites most of all.[25]

Canada too has built a number of dams, like the Peace River and Bow-Saskatchewan projects, but there is no equivalent of the Bureau of Reclamation in that country, nor anything like the hydraulic civilization that has appeared south of the border along the Colorado, Missouri, or Columbia rivers. There has not been much of an aridity problem there either. Aside from the little patch known as Palliser's Triangle, which is not truly arid, Canada's West has not required so profound an adjustment to the problem of dryness.

Nonetheless, nature has played a powerful role in the pace and success of development in western Canada just as it has in the western United States. Up there, the great obstacle to an agricultural empire has come more from a high latitude and a short growing season rather than a lack of moisture, but the obstacle has been intensely real all the same.[26] With the annexation of Rupert's Land in 1870, an immense country seemed suddenly available for rural development. Toronto elites imagined a future West that would be the home of a hundred million people, that would surpass the country to the south in size, stability, enlightenment, and prosperity, that would become the world centre of an invigorated British Empire. As Doug Owram has shown, that unbounded optimism began to disintegrate by the mid-1880s, as it came under attack by disillusioned westerners themselves. In Owram's words, "the great partnership which was supposed to develop between the metropolitan centre and the hinterland was rejected by the hinterland even before it had been fully formed."[27] Ever since that first moment of reassessment, western Canadians have doubted that the eastern provinces really understand their situation – the hard, physical reality of creating a life on the prairies and in the mountains – or sympathize as much as they should. Subsequently, the Canadian West went on to seek a separate identity, more local control over its resources, and a closer fit to the land. To be sure, much settlement occurred after those dark days of the 1880s and 1890s; so-called "improved land" in Manitoba, Saskatchewan, and Alberta increased from less than three hundred thousand acres in 1881 to nearly sixty million acres in 1931.[28] However, as impressive an achievement as this expansion was, it never represented a great imperial power base.

Still another way in which development had to be radically rethought came from land ownership in the West. The original idea in the United States was that development involved turning all the land into fee-simple private property, bounded by sturdy fences, from the East Coast all the way to the West Coast. That plan broke down; it did not get over the Rocky Mountains intact. Thirty years after President Abraham Lincoln signed the Homestead Act, a monument to the private property ideal, another Congress gave another president the authority to withdraw lands from entry to safeguard vulnerable watersheds and secure a timber supply.[29] That act, which Marion Clawson and Burnell Held have called "one of the most important land administration measures ever undertaken in the United States," eventually led to a national forest system covering nearly two hundred million acres.[30] In the 1930s virtually all homesteading, and thus all further settlement of the public domain, came to an end, leaving much of the West in the hands of the federal government. Today, the federal government owns approximately one-third of the entire nation, making it the country's biggest landowner by far and the dominant power over national as well as western development. In some western states as much as 50 or even 80 per cent of the land is public domain.[31]

Again, the impetus behind this change in course came partly from nature. The same environmental conditions that made federal water projects necessary, if agriculture was to succeed, required the preserving of watersheds from deforestation by private timber companies. Lands that could not be irrigated could not be homesteaded; therefore, they could not become fee-simple rural estates. Most of the public domain lies where nature has made the land too dry or too cold for agricultural settlement. What is more important is that these extraordinary changes in American land policy came about because of dramatic changes in peoples' attitudes toward private land ownership, and indeed toward the whole capitalist logic of development. By the 1890s many citizens had begun to worry about where that logic was leading – to a landscape depleted and degraded, they feared, by frontier exploiters and metropolitan businessmen.

We call this reaction the conservation movement and note that it grew out of outrage over the decline of American forests and wildlife. Organizations like the Audubon Society and the Sierra Club appeared in those years that produced the first land withdrawals, and they supported a permanent federal responsibility for controlling the effects of unbridled development. No one contemplating the West in 1869, when the first trains began running triumphantly across the continent, foresaw any of this change in public mood, any more than they understood the limits of the western land itself. They could not have imagined the intense reaction against privatization and exploitation of land that would begin to flare up within a few decades; nor foresee a future West perpetually under the management of federal resource agencies. The idea of federal subsidies to railroad construction was a familiar idea, but not a vast federal ownership and management of the land in perpetuity.

The Canadian government took a strikingly different course in land ownership, one that I believe has never received sufficient attention by historians in either country. Ottawa did not remain the major landowner in the Canadian West; in the North, it did, but not in the West. In 1930, the federal government turned over all its lands, except a few parks, to the western provinces. For the previous sixty years those lands had been federal property, the so-called "Crown lands," acquired from the Hudson's Bay Company in 1870. British Columbia was an exception to that pattern; its Crown lands became the provincial government's responsibility immediately upon joining the Confederation.[32] As other provinces formed, they too wanted the same local control over resources that British Columbia exercised, but for a long time their pleas were ignored. The "National Policy" of development, directed from far-away Ottawa, allowed the Prairie provinces little say about railroad grants, agricultural settlement, or timber and mineral extraction. In 1930 that situation abruptly shifted. Ottawa proclaimed that it had fulfilled its major development goals in the West and handed over its huge estate to Winnipeg, Regina, and Edmonton.[33]

Exactly the same case could have been made in the American West, and around 1930 it was indeed being made, impatiently and stridently, by western state governors. They could claim the same kind of precedent as their counterparts to the north, for the states to the East, as well as the state of Texas among their own number, had not become or remained federal property for very long. But despite strenuous arguments, no handover occurred. The American public would not let it occur, then or at any time thereafter. They wanted to leave the federal government in charge of those acres simply because they trusted it more than they trusted the western states, with their open-door attitudes toward mining and timber companies. New attitudes had emerged that encouraged American public leaders to break a very old precedent, disappointing many westerners, and to assume a permanent resource stewardship in the West.

Why did such a federal responsibility emerge in the United States but not in Canada? Were the provinces such good resource stewards that the question of who to trust was never an issue? I doubt that such was the case.[34] One has only to look at the controversial record of British Columbia, where conservationists have severely criticized the cozy relation between the Ministry of Forestry and private timber companies, to see that there was reason enough to worry. The issue of conservation, however, does not seem to have even come up in Canada in 1930. The most plausible reason for that silence is that conservation was a less potent political movement in that country than in the United States, for reasons of culture and politics that invite further research. Quite tellingly, there were at the time almost no popular conservation organizations north of the forty-ninth parallel – nothing like America's Sierra Club and the rest – to stir up debate over issues of land and conservation. In contrast, such a debate had been going on in the United States since the 1890s, and it explains why a strong federal responsibility over land emerged and why it continues down to this very day. Even as angry Sagebrush Rebels demand cession of the public domain to the states and its privatization, environmental groups like the Wilderness Society and Earth First! still fight for federal ownership.

Obviously, the federal land managers in the United States have not lived up to all of those early rosy expectations. These days they are the target of as much criticism as timber or mining companies, and for many Americans the government no longer seems to be the safe guardian of the public lands it once was. Moreover, conservation expectations themselves have changed from the late nineteenth century to the present, and changed unpredictably. A few decades back the Forest Service could not have foreseen the degree to which its historic sense of mission would be criticized by a post World War II environmental movement. Instead of aiming merely for a sustainable harvest, they now must learn to apply ecological science to land-use decisions. They must protect old-growth forests, endangered species, and millions of acres of wilderness, which was not part of their original responsibility. Nor, for that matter, do any of these conservation demands of today fit easily into the traditional logic of capitalism. Where then did they originate? From a rising affluence, which is to say from the very success of capitalism? Or do they stem from deeper cultural shifts – from fears and anxieties about the course of development and progress – that have produced a powerful challenge to capitalism? We do not really know the answer.

It is time to sum up the argument I have been making. Traditionally, both American and Canadian historians agreed that modern capitalism was where social evolution was taking us, yet both professed to find in the North American environment a powerful counterforce that gave each nation a distinctive identity in the world. Then the historians, along with government and business leaders, ran up against environmental challenges in the movement west, challenges that forced the course of development into deviations that became regions. Changing cultural attitudes toward development itself, toward capitalism, and toward conservation, also forced deviations from the norm. The outcome of all those unanticipated events is a continent of diversities. The North America we see today is not the outcome of a simple linear process. Its history reveals natural obstacles that no amount of logic or technology could fully overcome, and cultural turns that we cannot easily explain.

According to the classical idea of development, nature can be transformed into almost anything the human mind desires. Deserts and mountains should mean nothing. Since capital is the same universalizing force everywhere, it should be nonsensical to talk about the need to adapt to nature. Moreover, a distinctive regional West in either Canada or the United States should make no sense. The world over should become nothing but an abstract, logical hierarchy of urban centres ruling over their producing hinterlands or peripheries – a series of neat concentric circles drawn by the hand of money. The historical picture of North America, however, along with that of other parts of the earth, has been far more complicated, far more interesting, than that.

Despite the homogenizing hand of capital, regions have taken shape, just as national differences have appeared and persisted. Thus, the Canadian West has not only become different from the Canadian East, in ways that none of the metropolitan historians ever fully understood, but also has become, although often in subtle ways, different from the American West.[35] The differences stem in part from different cultural legacies brought into these two regions, but they also come from the inescapable truth that nature differs from place to place; it is not one unbroken thing, a single grand enemy to be defeated. Nature differs from east to west, and it differs from north to south. Those differences are most obvious around the Great Lakes: the Precambrian Shield lies to the north, creating a Canada of thin soil, rich forests, and mineral wealth, while on the American side a fertile savannah has given way to the corn belt, a landscape of incomparable agricultural productivity. Differences exist in the West too, and indeed they can be found from sea to shining sea.

According to the German writer Wolfgang Sachs, the idea of development "stands today like a ruin in an intellectual landscape, an outdated monument to an immodest era."[36] Whatever coherence it once had, it no longer enjoys, unless one defines it merely as increasing the gross domestic product. Once development suggested that there was, or there must be, a single cultural standard by which all people could be measured – essentially, a standard of living defined by nations like the United States, Canada, or England, and by the metropolises within those nations. No longer is that so, as people everywhere have begun to reject the notion of a single standard, for to accept such a notion would be to denigrate their history, their achievement, their cultural uniqueness. Even as a merely economic norm the idea of development is becoming more unacceptable, for it teaches an outmoded ethos of unlimited materialism and accumulation, claiming that such an ethos is a universal need or drive found among all people. Those who have questioned the universality of that ethos are, by the logic of development, irrational. Now, however, the doubters are increasing, and they have on their side all the generations who lived before the invention of development, all those who still live outside the development myth today, along with many of the great philosophers and moral teachers in history. Today the critics charge that the myth of development perpetuates exploitative attitudes toward nature, attitudes that are responsible for the global environmental crisis we find ourselves in. They say that the myth has brought problems as well as benefits, and that what it calls its benefits have often been temporary, fragile, and extremely costly in ecological terms.

Historians must agree with development's critics at least to this extent: as an idea organizing our study of the past it has not been very reliable. It has not given us a clear picture of the losses as well as gains, the failures as well as successes, the surprises that we have experienced over time. It has not accounted for the emergence of important national *and* regional differences that defy simple models or theories about a linear course of progress. Nature, we can see more clearly today than a few years back, has been a powerful, volatile force in our lives, complex beyond our understanding, never fully conquered despite all the capital, expertise, and technology we have deployed. Culture also has been an unfathomable, unpredictable force, capable of abrupt shifts in mood and value. The complicated history of nature interacting with culture in North America has made a shambles of development as a myth, as an ideology, as a program of action, and as a story to tell our children.

Notes

1   A provocative discussion of these themes appears in William G. Robbins, *Colony and Empire: The Capitalist Transformation of the American West* (Lawrence: University Press of Kansas, 1994), chapter 3. Robbins tends to see Canada as less aggressive toward its native peoples than the United Slates, a view some observers might dispute.

2   Gustavo Esteva, "Development," in *The Development Dictionary: A Guide to Knowledge and Power*, Wolfgang Sachs, ed. (London: Zed Books, 1992), 9.

3   H. W. Arndt, "Economic Development: A Semantic History," *Economic Development and Social Change* 29 (April 1981), 461.

4   By the late-nineteenth century the United States saw itself, and was so seen by many others, as the quintessential developed nation, essentially capitalistic but blending elements of socialism and populism. A stimulating account of this era of emergence is Martin J. Sklar, *The United States as a Developing Country: Studies in U.S. History in the Progressive Era and the 1920s* (New York: Cambridge University Press, 1992).

5   Frederick Jackson Turner, "The Significance of the Frontier in American History" [1893], *Frontier and Section: Selected Essays of Frederick Jackson Turner*, Ray Alien Billington, ed. (Englewood Cliffs, NJ: Prentice-Hall, 1961), 37.

6   Turner, "Significance of the Frontier," 38.

7   "Today," Turner wrote, "we are looking with shock upon a changed world." The best he could offer were hollow, half-hearted words: "Let us hold to our attitude of faith and courage. Let us dream as our fathers dreamt and let us make our dreams come true." In "The West and American Ideals" [1914], *Frontier and Section*, 106.

8   Among the sources I have drawn on here are J. M. S. Careless, "Frontierism, Metropolitanism", 21; Ramsay Cook, "Frontier and Metropolis: The Canadian Experience," in *The Maple Leaf Forever: Essays on Nationalism and Politics in Canada* (Toronto: Macmillan, 1971), 166–75; Carl Berger, *The Writing of Canadian History: Aspects of English-Canadian Historical Writing since 1900*, 2d ed. (Toronto: University of Toronto Press, 1986), esp. 174–78; W. L. Morton, "Clio in Canada: The Interpretation of Canadian History," *University of Toronto Quarterly* 15 (April 1946), 227–34; Carl Berger, "William Morton: The Delicate Balance of Region and Nation," in *The West and the Nation: Essays in Honor of W.L. Morton*, Carl Berger and Ramsay Cook, eds. (Toronto; McClelland and Stewart, 1976), 9–32. The continuing appeal of the metropolitan school of thought is demonstrated by the various essays in *Heartland and Hinterland: A Geography of Canada*, 2d ed., L. D. McCann, ed. (Scarborough, ON: Prentice-Hall Canada, 1987).

9   On the forest staple, see A. R. M. Lower, *The North American Assault on the Canadian Forest: A History of the Lumber Trade between Canada and the United States* (Toronto: Ryerson Press, 1938); and *Great Britain's Woodyard: British American and the Timber Trade, 1763–1867* (Montreal: McGill-Queen's University Press, 1973).

10   Innis, *The Fur Trade in Canada,*, 401–2. See also Abraham Rotstein, "Innis: The Alchemy of Fur and Wheat," *Journal of Canadian Studies* 12 (Winter 1977), 6–31; and William Christian, "The Inquisition of Nationalism," ibid., 52–72. The similarity of Innis's work to modern dependency theory is the theme of Mel Watkins's "The Staple Theory Revisited," ibid., 83–95.

11   See D. G. Creighton, *The Commercial Empire of the St. Lawrence*. Creighton's "environmentalism" consisted of a great river system inspiring economic development, giving as it were nature's approval to commerce. In the midst of a panegyric to the St. Lawrence he wrote: "From the river there rose, like an exhalation, the dream of western commercial empire."

12   The reaction to Turner's thesis is summarized in Michael S. Cross, ed., *The Frontier Thesis and the Canadas: The Debate on the Impact of the Canadian Environment* (Toronto: Copp Clark, 1970). Most authorities seem to concur that the staple school (or Laurentian, or metropolitan – the names seem to be interchangeable) was influenced by Turner, but not in terms of explaining the origins of democracy. See also George F. G. Stanley, "Western Canada and the Frontier Thesis," *Canadian Historical Association Report* (Toronto: University of Toronto Press, 1940), 105–14; Paul F. Sharp, "Three Frontiers: Some Comparative Studies of Canadian, American, and Australian Settlement," *Pacific Historical Review* 24 (November 1955), 369–77; Robin Fisher, "Duff and George Go West: A Tale of Two Frontiers," *Canadian Historical Review* 68 (December 1987), 501–28; and Winks, *The Relevance of Canadian History*, 14, 21.

13   Much of Cronon's book seems to be an application of ideas first laid out by J. M. S. Careless in "Metropolis and Region: The Interplay between City and Region in Canadian History before 1914," *Urban History Review* (1978), 99–118. "Behind the rise of frontier, hinterland or region in Canada," writes Careless, "lay the power of the metropolis, which ultimately disposed of their resource harvest, strongly fostered their expansion, and widely controlled their very existence."

14   William J. Cronon, *Nature's Metropolis: Chicago and the Great West* (New York: W.W. Norton, 1991), 46–54.

15   Ibid., 85.

16   These two Wests include, of course, many diversities, as Jean Barman has argued in "The West Beyond the West: The Demography of Settlement in British Columbia," *Journal of Canadian Studies* 25 (fall 1990), 5–18.

17   The best guide to this subject is John A. Eagle, *The Canadian Pacific Railway and the Development of Western Canada, 1896–1914* (Kingston, ON: McGill-Queen's University Press, 1989). A splendid visual guide is Bill McKee and Georgeen Klassen, *Trail of Iron: The CPR and the Birth of the West, 1880–1930* (Vancouver: Douglas and McIntyre, 1983).

18   Kenneth H. Norrie, "The National Policy and the Rate of Prairie Settlement," *Journal of Canadian Studies* 14 (fall 1979), 63–76.

19   This is not to deny that there were many ways in which Canada looked south for a model, if only out of self-defence; see Richard Preston, ed. *The Influence of the*

United States on Canadian Development: Eleven Case Studies (Durham, NC: Duke University Press, 1972).

20   C. J. Trade, "Ethnicity and the Prairie Environment: Patterns of Old Colony Mennonite and Doukhobor Settlement," in *Man and Nature on the Prairies*, Richard Alien, ed., Canadian Plains Studies 6 (Regina, Sask.: Canadian Plains Research Center, 1976), 46–65.

21   David H. Breen, *The Canadian Prairie West and the Ranching Frontier, 1874–1924* (Toronto: University of Toronto Press, 1983), 125–27; and the same author's "The Turner Thesis and the Canadian West: A Closer Look at the Ranching Frontier," in *Essays on Western History*, Lewis H. Thomas, ed. (Edmonton: University of Alberta Press, 1976), 147–58.

22   That a conservative like Robert Borden would support nationalization of railroads would be unthinkable in the United States. See John A. Eagle, "Sir Robert Borden, Union Government and Railway Nationalization," *Journal of Canadian Studies* 10 (November 1975), 59–66.

23   Turner, "Problems in American History" (1892), *Frontier and Section*, 30.

24   Ray Allen Billington, *Frederick Jackson Turner: Historian, Scholar, Teacher* (New York: Oxford University Press, 1973), 213–14. Turner read Powell's 1896 essay, "Physiographic Regions of the United States," and thereafter began working on a "sectional" interpretation of American history, though it never achieved quite the impact that his frontier thesis had.

25   The literature on western water development is growing rapidly. For a recent overview of the environmental problems it has created, see Marc Reisner, *Cadillac Desert: The American West and Its Disappearing Water* (New York: Viking, 1986); and for historical perspectives, see Norris Hundley Jr., *The Great Thirst: Californians and Water, 1770s–1990s* (Berkeley: University of California Press, 1992); Donald Pisani, *To Reclaim a Divided West: Water, Law, and Public Policy, 1848–1902* (Albuquerque: University of New Mexico Press, 1992); and my own *Rivers of Empire: Water, Aridity, and the Growth of the American West* (New York: Oxford University Press, 1995), and "Water as a Tool of Empire," in *An Unsettled Country: Changing Landscapes of the American West* (Albuquerque: University of New Mexico Press, 1994), 31–54.

26   A fine study of Alberta settlement, with a shrewd discussion of the interactive role of the metropolis, the frontier, and the environment, is Paul Voisey, *Vulcan: The Making of a Prairie Community* (Toronto: University of Toronto Press, 1988). See also Max Gerhart Geier, "A Comparative History of Rural Community on the Northwest Plains: Lincoln County Washington, and the Wheatland Region, Alberta, 1880–1930," Ph.D. thesis, Washington State University, 1990.

27   Doug Owram, *Promise of Eden: The Canadian Expansionist Movement and the Idea of the West, 1856–1900* (Toronto: University of Toronto Press, 1980), 220. Also, on the rise of a western identity see R. Douglas Francis, "From Wasteland to Utopia: Changing Images of the Canadian West in the Nineteenth Century," *Great Plains Quarterly 7* (summer 1987), 178–94; and "In Search of a Prairie Myth: A

Survey of the Intellectual and Cultural Historiography of Prairie Canada," *Journal of Canadian Studies* 24 (fall 1989), 44–69.

28   R. W. Murchie, assisted by William Alien and J. F. Booth, *Agricultural Progress on the Prairie Frontier*, vol. 5, Canadian Frontiers of Settlement series (Toronto: Macmillan, 1936), 8.

29   On March 3, 1891, Congress passed the Forest Reserve Act, authorizing the President to reserve forested lands from the public domain. An earlier reservation of land took place in 1872, with the creation of Yellowstone National Park as "a public park or pleasuring ground for the benefit and enjoyment of the people."

30   Marion Clawson and Burnell Held, *The Federal Lands: Their Use and Management* (Lincoln: University of Nebraska Press, 1957), 28. The Americans had, in effect, to reinvent an institution of public ownership that was never discarded in Canada. See H. V. Nelles, *The Politics of Development: Forests, Mines, and Hydro-Electric Power in Ontario, 1849–1941* (Hamden, CT: Archon Books, 1974), 2–9.

31   The most recent figures appear in U.S. Department of Interior, Bureau of Land Management, *Public Land Statistics 1990*, vol. 175 (Washington, DC: Government Printing Office, 1991).

32   See Robert E. Cail, *Land, Man, and the Law: The Disposal of Crown Lands in British Columbia, 1871–1913* (Vancouver: University of British Columbia Press, 1974), which is mainly about the wise leadership of Governor James Douglas in forming a provincial land policy.

33   An old but still valuable discussion of this issue is Chester Martin, *"Dominion Lands" Policy*, which comprises the second half of the second volume of the Canadian Frontiers of Settlement series, edited by W. A. Mackintosh and W. L. G. Joerg (Toronto: Macmillan, 1938). See especially chapter 12, which deals with the transfer of 1930. Martin was a strong provinces-rights advocate, particularly for Manitoba. For a general review of federal policy, see Kirk N. Lambrecht, *The Administration of Dominion Lands, 1810–1930* (Regina, Sask.: Canadian Plains Research Center, 1991).

34   According to John Herd Thompson and Alien Seager, "the attitude of the federal government, Liberal or Conservative, to resource development did not differ significantly from that of the provinces." In *Canada, 1922–1939: Decades of Discord* (Toronto: McClelland and Stewart, 1985), 84.

35   This is also the argument of Gerald Friesen in "The Prairie West since 1945: A Historical Survey," in *The Making of the Modern West: Western Canada since 1945*, A. W. Rasporich, ed. (Calgary: University of Calgary Press, 1984), 1–10; and in Friesen, *The Canadian Prairies: A History* (Lincoln: University of Nebraska Press, 1984), 466. Friesen, however, places more emphasis on local economic control than on environmental adaptation. Maurice Careless has also noted the growth and persistence of regional identities in Canada, but he tends to emphasize racial and ethnic identities over environmentally-based ones, which may reflect his Ontario-Quebec background. See his "'Limited Identities' in Canada," *Canadian Historical Review* 50 (March 1969), 1–10. Finally, William Westfall writes on the

growing interest in regional studies in "On the Concept of Region in Canadian History and Literature," *Journal of Canadian Studies* 15 (summer 1980), 3–15, though he too dismisses environmental factors in history as irrelevant. It is unclear to me why stressing cultural factors only should be considered less reductive or simplistic.

36   Wolfgang Sachs, "On the Archaeology of the Development Idea," *The Ecologist* 20 (March/April 1990), 42. See also his "Global Ecology and the Shadow of' Development," in *Global Ecology: A New Arena of Political Conflict*, Sachs, ed. (London: Zed Books, 1993), 3–21.

Chapter 3

From 54°40' to Free Trade: Relations between the American Northwest and Western Canada[1]

Gerald Friesen, University of Manitoba

Canada's 1988 federal election, which was called just after my visit to Washington State University, and the Free Trade Agreement between Canada and the United States, which was due to be implemented on January 1, 1989, established the context in which this lecture was delivered. During my conversations and lectures at Washington State, I suggested that the adoption of the Canadian-American trade treaty, which was extended to include Mexico in the North American Free Trade Agreement (NAFTA, 1993), would change the relations between the two countries. The following brief survey of trans-border regional history illustrated my belief that the new circumstances would require patience and understanding from citizens on both sides of the boundary.

When the lecture was delivered, Canadians were anticipating a heated debate in the general election campaign over whether to approve the Free Trade Agreement. I had just heard from a friend in the advertising industry about a rumoured script being prepared for a national party television advertisement. According to this report, the camera would approach two well-dressed men seated across from each other at a table littered with paper, including one neatly-stacked pile about a foot high (the actual trade agreement); they are clearly at the end of a difficult but successful negotiation. One says to the other, in an unmistakable American accent, that there was only one further line he wanted to change and the deal could be wrapped up; his counterpart replies that that could certainly be accommodated – one line would pose no problem. The camera then zooms in on the paper between the two men to reveal a map of North America, where the American is erasing the boundary line between Canada and the United States. A version of the advertisement did, indeed, figure in the election campaign.

Whether for or against the trade deal, Canadians genuinely believed that their nation was at a crossroads in 1988. True, no political leader has ever entered a campaign declaring that the election about to be contested is irrelevant. But there was something different about the atmosphere in the autumn of that year. I thought then that historical understanding should also be a part of the public debate. This is why it seemed appropriate to ask what light might be cast on contemporary affairs by the history of the Northwest.

An American reader might be interested in a few words of explanation about why a mere tariff reduction measure should seem so important to a modern nation of thirty million people. I suggest that, buried in the Canadian psyche along with Mountie uniforms and hockey, are two fears about North America's structure and destiny. The first is that continental economic forces are well-nigh irresistible and that the continent must eventually be shaped into a single, regionally specialized, productive unit. The second, slightly different in approach, is that the dominant communications media of a given era might permit the survival of only one political entity north of Mexico.

An article published in the *Times* of London in 1866 and reprinted some months later in Northwest Canada illustrates the fear of economic integration. The article advocated the sale of Canada's Northwest to the United States, just as Alaska was about to be sold, because the newly reunited American federation was prepared to offer the then proprietor, the Hudson's Bay Company, a higher price than could the Canadian government. The business column in the *Times* went on:

... patriotism, like philanthropy, in business is rarely anything more than a pretence, and is nearly always a mistake. If the Americans can turn the territory to better account than our own people for the great use of mankind, it is desirable that they should be permitted to do so; and in any case, it is certain that all political attempts to prevent the country from being settled by those who are best adapted for the work must, by rendering perpetual irritation, prove worse than futile.

Naturally, Canadians resented this argument, but the declaration, along with the Canadian reaction, neatly captures one Canadian perspective on the future of northern North America: economic forces override political decisions, willy-nilly, and there is nothing that anyone can do to sidetrack businessmen determined to follow this inexorable logic. As a famous Canadian tract of the 1960s, George Grant's *Lament for a Nation*, declared, "No small country can depend for its existence on the loyalty of its capitalists."

The second Canadian fear is also based partly on perceptions of the geography of the continent, but its emphasis rests on the perception that communications technology may subvert historic cultural and political loyalties. It is evident that adjoining regions of Canada and the United States are remarkably similar; by referring to physical maps of the continent, one might conclude that, but for historical accident, this vast land mass should be divided quite differently or, indeed, should belong to a single country. This observation periodically raises doubts in Canadian hearts, doubts expressed most bluntly and forcefully by a transplanted British scholar then living in Toronto, Goldwin Smith, in his famous book, now almost a hundred years old, *Canada and the Canadian Question*. The first sentence warned readers that, if they wanted "to know what Canada is," they should begin by turning from the political to the physical map. The political map displays a large united land; the physical map displays "four separate projections of the cultivable and habitable part of the Continent into arctic waste." The four parts were the Maritimes, Old [Central] Canada, the Northwest [Prairies], and British Columbia. Each was divided from the others "by great barriers of nature, wide and irreclaimable wildernesses or manifold chains of mountains" and each was "closely connected by nature, physically and economically" with the adjoining American region. Thus, Smith concluded,

> Whether the four blocks of territory constituting the Dominion can forever
> be kept by political agencies united among themselves and separate from their
> Continent of which geographically, economically, and with the exception of
> Quebec, ethnologically, they are parts, is the Canadian question.

Smith had expressed a second fundamental Canadian worry: that is, that there is not only an economic reason for continental unity but a logic, a "natural" destiny, rooted in geography and communications.

Assumptions about geography, communications, and economics went to the heart of the free trade debate in 1988. Supporters of the trade deal argued that business must be free to respond to global economic changes and that, anyway, Canada is a natural partner of the United States because the two nations "share a continent." Opponents consistently raised the same arguments but perceived them as threats: continental economic unity would destroy a distinctive nation and require North American political and cultural unity in all but name. The free trade discussion of 1988 was not a minor episode in Canadian life. Citizens took the election seriously because they believed their decision went to the very heart of national existence.

If one turns to a cartographical collection to survey cross-border regional history, one discovers not only that knowledge about this district changed during recent centuries, but that *location itself is relative*. We understand where we are situated (note Northrop Frye's suggestion that the appropriate Canadian question is "where is here?"), by reference to *other* places, and thus to the *relations* between sites. Changes in resource use, trade patterns, communications technology, diplomatic and military alignments, even in national will, can alter our *location* as they change our perceptions of geography. About a hundred and fifty years ago, American and British map-makers disagreed on the hue of northwest North America; as recently as the 1920s, Canadian military strategists planned that Canadian troops should lay siege to Seattle and thereby defend Canada from its only perceived external threat. These present boundaries, these places that we think of as permanent, are not fixed and immutable.

In any cartographical survey of the American Northwest and Canadian West, four patterns or configurations seem to crystallize. The first reflects an era of Aboriginal dominance. This pattern is evident long after Europeans had settled and "claimed" the continent. The second pattern expresses the impact of European trading empires which became evident in the seventeenth century and imposed itself upon the territory during the closing decades of the eighteenth and early decades of the nineteenth century. One product of the French-British-Spanish contest was the emergence of a new power, the United States. A third pattern reflects the development of European and American industrial capitalism, and stretches from the middle of the nineteenth to the mid-twentieth century. In this era the lines that we recognize as familiar were drawn on maps, including the national and state boundaries, rail networks, local road systems, and land surveys. A fourth pattern illustrates the global re-orientation of military and cultural power that commenced during World War II, when not only the international balance of power began to shift, but so did the *types of lines* that defined our places on the map, whether microwaves, pipe-lines, satellite transmissions of television signals, or football team loyalties.

Lying behind this categorization of the region's cartography is a caricature of modern history. Rough and ready though it is, this model asserts, first, the primacy in regional history of European contact with North America's Aboriginal people; second, the influence of European capitalism and literacy on the course of world history; third, the central place of nations during the nineteenth and twentieth centuries; and, fourth, that the events of the last four or five decades have created a world sufficiently different in kind to warrant a distinctive pattern in regional cartography.

The distance between Aboriginal and European cultures in northwest America was wide in some respects, narrow in others. The technology that enabled the Europeans to contemplate a global empire – especially the technology of communications – was indeed outside the experience of the Aboriginal people. However, within the North American continent, Europeans relied on Aboriginal knowledge of the terrain and Aboriginal technological adaptations. Europeans did not challenge Aboriginal sovereignty in the northwestern districts of North America during the seventeenth and eighteenth centuries.

The two cultures, Aboriginal and European, defined the political territory, as opposed to its cultural dimensions, in comparable fashion. The

1801 "ak ki mo ki map" was built around the Great Divide in the Rocky Mountains: two worlds shared this part of the continent, one focused on the Columbia and looking coastward, one focused on the Missouri and looking toward the plains. European maps of the same era introduced another demarcation, one that separated the northern from the southern plains. Thus, in addition to the distinction between the Great Plains and the Pacific coast, they also divided the Saskatchewan-Churchill river system draining into Hudson Bay from the Missouri-Mississippi system flowing to the Gulf.

Neither of the two regional maps – one European, one Aboriginal – is superior to the other. As the Canadian economist Harold Innis recognized, both relied heavily on the river systems as routes of communication. Innis added that the river systems, in conjunction with the dominant staple export goods, eventually established the boundaries of distinct national communities: "The northern half of North America remained British," he wrote, "because of the importance of fur as a staple product." Surely this, written in 1930, was an early and effective answer to Goldwin Smith's observations on the natural destiny created by the north-south currents in the geography and economy of North America. It was also a declaration of the continuing autonomy of a Northwest region within the international trading system. Global trade in the seventeenth and eighteenth centuries had not dislocated the native cultures of Northwest America. The two civilizations, Aboriginal and European, lived in juxtaposition. Neither controlled nor dictated the nature and pace of change of the other. But, as Innis noted, the experience with fur as an export staple influenced the historical trajectory of actors living north of the forty-ninth parallel.

Was there a type of regional unity within the northwestern segment of America? Surely the answer is no. The native political and trade map featured numerous divisions, especially the line of the Rocky Mountains that distinguished groups east and west. The European map was divided between corporate empires and, of course, after 1818 and 1846, by political ambitions associated with government policy in the United States, Mexico, and Great Britain as well as British North America.

A third pattern developed during the nineteenth and first half of the twentieth century. It was shaped by the industrial capitalist economic system which spread from England to Europe and America and then around the globe. This trading and financial system imposed new pressures on the relatively empty fertile zones of the world. By displacing native peoples, European immigrants could, in turn, establish settler capitalist economies to satisfy their homelands' demand for food and raw materials. The struggle for control of these so-called empty lands – in Australia, South America, southern Africa, and western North America – produced comparable episodes in every zone: conflict with native people, struggles for control of the terms of trade, the emergence of railway corporations as central instruments of development, and, in certain districts, border problems. In North America, control of the boundary became a political issue. Today's residents of Washington state will be familiar with the 1844 presidential campaign slogan of "54°40' or fight" – the American claim that the boundary with the British colonies should be located in what is now central British Columbia. Americans may not be as familiar with the fact that this contest did not end in the 1840s. Nor was it truly settled when the newly united Canada (the British North America Act linked Ontario, Quebec, Nova Scoria, and New Brunswick in 1867) negotiated the admission of the western interior (1870) and British Columbia (1871) to the federation. Indeed, Canadians continued to worry about the fate of "their" West, and their alternative to the American national dream, to the end of the nineteenth century.

The Alaska boundary dispute, which erupted at the turn of the century, illustrated this deep anxiety among Canadians. It was believed in Canada that the United States would always attempt to ride roughshod over its northern neighbour and that the British government, when put to the test, preferred to mollify the Americans, even if, as in the case of the Alaskan panhandle, Canada's interests must be sacrificed.

Trade interests dominated these battles. Canadian leaders believed that, if American manufacturing companies dominated the economy of the northwest interior, and shipped via American routes in American conveyors, Canadian national sovereignty over these districts would soon be lost. Only the Canadian "National Policy" protective tariff of 1879, the extraordinary effort to build the Canadian Pacific transcontinental rail line in the 1880s, and the efforts to settle the prairies under Canadian supervision in the next three decades ensured that Canada retained its western empire, according to this view. As late as the 1890s, when American mine and rail promoters tried to exploit several mineral discoveries in the Kootenay region for their own advantage, the battle still raged. In response, the Canadian government underwrote an expensive rail project (the Crow's Nest Pass line), in order to ensure that the British Columbia mining towns traded with and shipped to Canadian rather than American businesses.

Many of the institutions established during the last half of the nineteenth century remain with us today. Indeed, in our daily lives, we still assume the fixity of the institutions that date from that era, including the international boundary. We assume that the two economies are relatively separate and distinct. We assume that, despite their friendship, the two countries march to different drummers, as they did during the two world wars. (Americans do not always understand the different Canadian perception of twentieth-century military history, in which the Canadian response was to join the British Empire/Commonwealth forces in August 1914 and September 1939, rather than entering the fray when the Americans did in April 1917 and December 7, 1941.)

While accepting these turn-of-the-century assumptions, residents of the continental Northwest have learned in recent years that economic forces have substantially changed the political environment. The oft-heard clichés about the heightened profile of the Pacific Rim emphasize the extraordinary shift in economic power in the last four decades. The steady trend to Western European unity, the collapse of the Soviet Union, and the growing economies of China and India are further evidence that the economic assumptions of the pre-1940 decades are gone forever.

Global economic reorientation has travelled on the wings of new technologies. Worldwide communications systems and transportation networks have created not just shifts in national power, but strides toward a global marketplace and even a global market-oriented culture. It should be no surprise that the "entertainment sector" – movies, music, television, and publishing – has become the second-largest export sector in the United States. Even the habits of consumerism are now standardized and exported. The very idea of a bumper sticker reading "Born to Shop" would have been outlandish in 1900, but the practice of "recreational shopping" exists today not just in Seattle but in Hong Kong and New Delhi; the so-called "mailing of America" has not stopped on the shores of this continent, but now circles the earth; and tourism – which of course is directly linked to these trends – has become a leading industry in many nations and is said to create one in nine jobs worldwide. More and more human activities are now allocated to the marketplace. Child care, weight loss, fitness, leisure, health: name the niche, advertise it, and soon it can be bought and sold, or refined into various levels of excellence and exclusivity.

The nature of employment is different today. At the turn of the century, two of every three prairie Canadians lived in rural areas and over half the prairie workforce worked in agriculture. In 1940, this proportion was still over 60 per cent rural, and 40 per cent of the workforce lived in farm households. Today, fewer than 20 per cent of prairie Canadians live on farms or in small towns and a smaller fraction – under 10 per cent – actually farm for a living. In that most rural of regions – according to our image of it – as in the rest of North America and Western Europe, two of every three jobs are now in the service (tertiary) sector. Health and education, government-sponsored social services, construction and transportation, retail and wholesale trade, food and lodging, real estate and finance, insurance and law, entertainment and consulting, computers and communications now constitute the job descriptions of a majority.

Changes in communications, work, and culture during the twentieth century suggest why we should regard the last fifty years as a distinct era in national and international history. The relations among the various regions of the globe have taken on a new aspect; the very means and types of self and community expression are different.

Global forces demand regional adaptations. As a consequence of the changed communications systems, the differences in the workforce, and the new circumstances in Asia, the very relations between the Canadian and American parts of the continental Northwest have altered. Most Canadians, especially in western Canada, are not aware of the magnitude of this departure. And yet, as the free trade debate intensified during the 1980s and 1990s, they heard repeatedly that 70 to 80 per cent of Canadian exports go to the United States and that about 70 per cent of Canadian imports come from the United States.

Surely this cannot be true for the West, they reply. Perhaps the central Canadian provinces of Ontario and Quebec are trading more with Americans? Perhaps it is Ontarians and Quebeckers who drive up the tourism deficit? Surely western Canadian export patterns have altered little in this century?

Such notions are wrong. Indeed, the United States has become far and away western Canada's largest export market – nearly twice as important as any other region of the world. The proportions are striking: the United States takes over half of the region's exports, Asia about one-fourth, and Western Europe 8 per cent. This marks an extraordinary change from the situation that prevailed as late as 1950.

The fundamental cause of this interdependence is the American quest for "safe" or "secure" energy supplies. The discovery of large quantities of crude oil and natural gas in Alberta (and, to a lesser degree, in Saskatchewan and British Columbia), combined with the exploitation of Canada's greatest natural resource, water (one-seventh of the world's supply of fresh water, and substantial production of hydroelectric power), has resulted in the shipment south of over $10 billion of oil, gas, and hydropower annually. Mining products, ranging from copper to uranium to potash, account for another $3 to $4 billion each year. Forestry is an equally large export industry and over $4 billion in forest products, notably softwood lumber and wood pulp, travelled south in the late 1980s. A number of smaller Canadian export industries also rely heavily on the American market, including fisheries, cattle and hogs (live, slaughtered, or processed), petrochemicals, steel products, distillery products, and clothing. In sum, Western Canada is dependent on the United States as an export market. This circumstance developed during the 1970s and 1980s, but Western Canadian recognition of the interdependence dawned only slowly.

The relations between the two regions offer another lesson in international trade. This lesson concerns American shipments to Canada. Washington and Idaho potatoes, California vegetables and fruits, Washington apples, western poultry and poultry products, northwest forest products and minerals are part of a longer list of "natural" products that, in the popular mind, constitute the bulk of trans-border transactions. To this catalogue one might add western Canadian purchases of southern textiles and clothing, midwest steel, petrochemicals and vehicles (including farm implements), and western computers, music, films, and airplanes. Western Canada buys handsome volumes of all these goods.

One additional area of this exchange, services, merits attention. When one considers that the service sector is the fastest-growing sector of the economy, it is surprising that one hears so little about the *exchange* of services. The Canadian government has predicted that almost all future job growth in the Canadian and American economies will be in the service sector. Moreover, the United States is the largest service producer and exporter in the world.

The United States provides $24 billion in services to Canadians; the reverse flow is about $11 billion (1988 estimates). The $35 billion total represents over 20 per cent of the total cross-border trade. Parts of this trade account are the normal consequences of such a gigantic bi-national exchange. For example, Canadian tourists run up a half-billion dollar deficit annually. The services category also includes freight and shipping, investment income, and dividends. None of these categories would cause one to pause. But another important sub-division within the services sector is business services – $5 billion in Canadian imports of American know-how, including the largest purchases of American television, publishing, and movies outside the United States itself.

By focusing on the exchange in the continental northwest, this brief commentary has not done justice to the cross-border traffic in eastern North America. The same pattern, an increasingly regionalized Canadian-American exchange, has developed there. Plants in Ontario ship goods across the border into New York, Ohio, and Michigan; Quebec sends products to New York and Massachusetts; the Atlantic provinces to New England. The northward flow is similarly regionalized. This is a very different continent from the one displayed on maps a century ago. The flow of trade and communications, in particular, is much closer to Goldwin Smith's "Canadian question" than one might have imagined. The changes in the global economy have had profound effects on regional life. The North American regions are aligned differently than they were even forty years ago.

What of nation and continent? How will the new technology and communications, and the addition of the FTA and NAFTA, affect northwestern American relations with western Canada? I believe that they will have a dramatic impact and that, to appreciate the point, one must refer to the history of Canada.

The desire for a separate nation in North America took root in the second half of the nineteenth century. It originated in the profound distinctiveness of French Catholic agrarian culture and, to a lesser degree, in the "loyalty" of those who rejected the American Revolution and then emigrated to Canada. It had its roots, too, in a separate economy that grew up within the Second British Empire (ca. 1784–1846), and in distinct business networks in fur, shipping, timber, and grain that perceived their interests to be different from those of American entrepreneurs. This cultural and economic foundation was reinforced when successive Canadian national governments implemented "national policies" between 1870 and 1930. Such policies have assumed mythical proportions in Canada partly because they were said to counteract an American challenge to Canadian sovereignty. Moreover, Canadian citizens' self-perception had more obvious European connections, especially French and English ties, than did the American, and its institutions of law and government (including the monarchy itself), all referred to the "Old Country" more fervently than was the case in the United States. By the turn of the twentieth century, Canadian separateness on the North American continent was a fact, confirmed dramatically in two national elections fought over free trade with the United States, in 1891 and 1911, when the dangers of the American tie were assessed and the "British connection" was affirmed.

While Canadians have inherited a nineteenth-century sense of separate nationhood – of a Canadian patriotism – the twentieth century has added to that separateness a difference in the Canadian and American perceptions of the role of the market or "free enterprise" in the shaping of public decisions and private lives. Even casual students of Canadian life are aware of the greater role of the state in the Canadian economy. The Canadian Pacific Railway was a joint achievement of government and a private corporation. Later, its two competitors were brought under government ownership as the Canadian National Railways. Until 1988, the national air carrier, Air Canada, was a publicly owned company. Many of the major utilities that provide Canadians with electricity and telephone service are, or once were, "crown-owned" corporations. The Canadian Broadcasting Corporation is similarly government-owned, and so are almost all hospitals and educational institutions. Medical insurance is prepaid, universal, compulsory, and state-supported from coast to coast, and so are seniors' pensions, child allowances, and unemployment insurance. These differences grew in importance in the decades after World War II and were brought into sharp relief for Canadians by the rhetoric and policies of the Reagan era. Despite apparent Canadian-American agreement on public policy, especially as voiced by Prime Minister Mulroney between 1984 and 1993, and by the Chrétien administrations (1993–97, 1997-2003), these contrasts remain important. For example, while the unionized proportion of the American workforce dropped below 18 per cent in the 1980s, the comparable Canadian proportion was about twice as high, around 35 to 38 per cent. In short, Canada has been much affected in recent decades by European currents of state capitalism, trade unionism, and social democracy. Canada's partial rejection of the iron law of the marketplace contrasts with American practice and American ideology. In the generation after 1945, Canada articulated a distinctive North American version of the just society.

To the nineteenth century inheritance of patriotic independence and the more recent strain of social justice I would like to add a third factor that resists the apparent transnational trend to homogeneity: culture. The term itself poses problems because we immediately translate it into the entertainment industry, on the one hand, or the arts, on the other. I mean it to include both but to mean neither: following Raymond Williams's definition, I propose that culture should be understood as the signifying practices – the signifying system – through which a social order or community meaning is communicated, reproduced, experienced, and explored. The process by which a community establishes its "signs" or hallmarks is always contested terrain. Corporate leaders in the United States have been particularly effective in this endeavour in the twentieth century as they have shipped around the globe an integrated vision of ideal government, "free" trade, and military superiority by means of "Rambo" and "Leave It to Beaver" and *Time* magazine. Most affected by the spillover from this, the single most powerful community signifying system in the world, was America's northern neighbour, Canada.

All expectations to the contrary, these cultural forces did not produce a uniform result or direction in Canada. Just as there are many Americans who do not subscribe entirely to the values of the dominant system, and criticize it from right or left, from religious or environmental or other assumptions, so there are many Canadians who dissent from one or another aspect of that American ideal. Canadians have found effective means of articulating these differences and asserting alternative visions of the community. Canadian "news" programs, fiction, short films, and scholarly writing have been especially influential expressions of this dissent. Taken together with the social democratic tradition and the nineteenth century patriotic determination to be "not American," this cultural resistance to continental and global centripetal force's can be labelled in derogatory fashion as merely Canadian nationalism, cultural elitism, or socialism. However, it is an important force in Canadian public life and in the expectations of Canadian citizens. Indeed, it shaped one of the most important political and cultural debates in the history of Canada, the 1988 election campaign on the free trade agreement.

This debate did not address an apolitical ideal, "free trade," but rather concerned a particular treaty draft and a substantial alteration of the fundamental relationship between what once were relatively distinct economies. The debate was made more complicated by the very global and regional forces of the last generation that have knit regions such as the two Northwests more closely together. The FTA and NAFTA address access to Canadian resources, especially energy and water, but also wood and minerals, which will be pivotal for both Canada and the United States in the twenty-first century. Not only the exchange of manufactured goods, but also, and even more important, despite all the protestations to the contrary, cultural products and services are affected by the treaty clauses. At bottom, the trade deal encourages Canadians to entrench "free-market forces," as Americans would define that phrase, in more aspects of their community life.

The fact that Canadians have been divided over whether the trade deal is a good or a bad idea is a rough measure of the state of Canadian culture. The popular vote in the 1988 general election was just slightly greater for parties opposed to the deal than for those in favour, though Canada's "first-past-the-post" electoral system based on geographical constituencies allocated the greatest number of seats to the free trade proponents. The global forces that have facilitated international capital flows, greater commodity trade, and broader cultural exchanges have pushed Canadians to accept more extensive use of the marketplace. The threat of economic unions elsewhere, notably in Europe but also in Asia, and of international trade wars, makes the North American harbour seem safe. Moreover, the interchange without restriction of certain commodities – petroleum, natural gas, fruits and vegetables, minerals, many manufactured goods – seems merely to build on the foundation of regional integration that grew increasingly important over the course of the twentieth century.

There is popular concern about these trends. The exchange of services across the international boundary opens the door to American-style, profit-driven private hospitals, personal care homes, and daycare facilities; how will they affect the corresponding Canadian systems? The exchange of manufactures puts enormous pressure on unions, as the Mexican "free-trade corridor" has demonstrated; how will NAFTA affect Canadian labour-management relations and the role of the state in such matters as the automatic check-off of union dues, the closed shop, and the minimum wage laws? Talk of trade in fresh water raises environmental concerns about the mixing of organisms from different drainage basins. The contentious clauses on cultural trade, which leave the door open to American penalties against Canadian "subsidies," may enshrine the American definition of culture and cultural goods in international law, thereby permitting the United States "entertainment industry" to establish what is meant by freedom of trade and what is a permissible restriction. Between the 1960s and the 1990s, Canada has relied on a battery of state measures to counteract the American cultural juggernaut, including the state-owned CBC and National Film Board, but also broadcast regulations, postal-rate assistance to serial publications, grants-in-aid of book publication, national preferences in taxes on advertising expenditures, and a variety of others. These rules interfere with the free flow of "commodities" and, thus, are subject to appeal, penalty, and eventual dismantling.

Canadians, like citizens of every country, are engaged in a continuous debate about the nature of the society in which they wish to live. At the close of the twentieth century, they are finding that the country's constituent regions – and the continent's constituent regions – are being knit together in new ways by changing trade and communications patterns as well as by different economic activities and cultural forces. Changing regional relationships and a different global context a *rethinking* of political arrangements.

When Canadians raise the spectre of "becoming American," as they often do in contemporary debates, they are saying that economics and communications are forcing them to reconsider the role of market forces and social legislation in their environment. They are saying that American needs, priorities, and collective choices are weighing ever more heavily in Canadians' own calculations. It is not that the lines and colours on the map are changing, necessarily, but that some of the circumstances which originally necessitated such diagrams no longer exist. It may be harder to map "Batman" and "Oprah" and *USA Today*, or to understand the lines that accompany private hospitals and non-union shops, but in a so-called global economy where the service sector provides most of the new jobs, such vehicles are pivotal instruments of cultural and political education. The challenges raised by the

London *Times* in 1866 and by Goldwin Smith in 1893 are once again requiring a Canadian response.

The greatest achievements in Canadian-American relations in the last hundred years have been a mutual reliance on the rule of law, and a willingness on the part of each partner to debate freely with the other. Now, as in the past, Americans are called upon to contend with, to study, and to assimilate a wide range of Canadian topics because many of the fields I have mentioned will become negotiating issues in continuing trade debates. The interregional relationship within the Northwest has changed forever. Just as global forces created new circumstances in the early seventeenth century, at the end of the eighteenth century, in the closing decades of the nineteenth century, so we are now living through a fourth decisive era of change in regional history. The Pacific Northwest and the Canadian West are at another turning point; but, this time, because global and regional changes have intersected, they force Canadians to reconsider their national loyalties and political ideals as well.

NOTE

1   This is a slightly revised version of the Pettyjohn lecture I delivered in 1988. I would like to thank Professors David Scratton and Margaret Andrews and the faculty and students at Washington State University for their gracious hospitality during my visit. I also wish to thank Professors Jacqueline Peterson and William Swageny, who did so much to make the visit possible and memorable.

Sources

Canada West Foundation. 1988. *The Effects of U.S. Protectionism on Western Canada*. Calgary.

———. 1988. *Export Opportunities: Analysis for the Western Canadian Economy*. Calgary

Department of Energy, Mines and Resources [Canada]. 1988. *Free Trade and Energy* Ottawa.

Economic Council of Canada. 1988. *Venturing Forth: An Assessment of the Canada-U.S. Trade Agreement*. Ottawa.

———. 1984. *Western Transition*. Ottawa.

Goetzmann, William H. 1988. *Looking at the Land of Promise: Pioneer Images of the Pacific North-west*. Pullman, WA: Washington State Univ. Press.

Governments of British Columbia, Alberta, Saskatchewan and Manitoba. 1979. *An Evaluation of the Impact of the Tokyo Round of the Multilateral Trade Negotiations on Western Canada*. n.p.

Grant, George. 1965. *Lament for a Nation: The Defeat of Canadian Nationalism*. Toronto: McLelland and Stewart.

Gwyn, Richard. 1985. *The 49th Paradox: Canada in North America*. Toronto: McClelland & Stewart.

Henderson, Michael D. ed. 1987. *The Future on the Table: Canada and the Free Trade Issue*. North York, ON: Masterpress.

Javorski, Mary. 1983. *The Canadian West Discovered: An Exhibition of Printed Maps from the 16th to Early 20th Centuries*. Calgary: Glenbow Museum.

Macmillan, Katie and Canada West Foundation. 1986. *Putting the Cards on the Table: Free Trade and Western Canadian Industries*. Calgary.

Phillips, Paul A. 1987. "Easternizing Manitoba: The Changing Economy of the New West." Unpublished manuscript. University of Manitoba.

Smith, Goldwin. 1891. *Canada and the Canadian Question*. London: Macmillan and Co.

Smith, Murray G. and Frank Stone, eds. 1987. *Assessing the Canada-U.S. Free Trade Agreement*. Halifax.

Stairs, Denis and Gilbert R. Winham, eds. 1985. *The Politics of Canada's Economic Relationship with the United States*. Royal Commission on the Economic Union and Development Prospects for Canada, Research Studies, vol. 29. Toronto.

Williams, Raymond. 1981. *A Vocabulary of Culture and Society*. Glasgow, Scotland: Fontana/Croom Helm.

Chapter 4

Sanctuary: Native Border Crossings and the North American West[1]

Beth LaDow

THE SIOUX, SITTING BULL, AND THE BORDER

The forty-ninth parallel boundary between western Canada and the United States appears like a quiet and unexplained guest in North American history, with its seemingly arbitrary straight line, slightly mysterious origin, and hazy significance, and to none more so than North America's Native peoples, whose territories it divided. Throughout the 1870s and 1880s the "medicine line," as many Native groups came to call the boundary, became, however briefly, their friend. As they were pushed and pulled across it, groups on both sides of the line saw in its "medicine" the hope of political refuge from the American or Canadian government on the other side. The first were the American Sioux, when suddenly in 1877 the American side meant exposure, pursuit, and captivity, and the Canadian side, sanctuary. Cross the line into the Great Mother's country and there was still hope of living as hunters rather than as the hunted. Cross it, said Robert Higheagle, a Sioux, and "[y]ou are altogether different. On one side you are perfectly free to do as you please. On the other you are in danger." It was a simple formula, less a tale of two nations than of one North American West, upon which history tells a story of variations (Higheagle, n.d.).

Their camp stretched along the west bank of Greasy Grass Creek in south central Montana, probably the largest off-reservation gathering of Indians ever seen. The Blackfeet, Hunkpapa, Ogalala, Sans Arc, Brule, and Minneconjous, and the Cheyenne, strung together like the segments of a caterpillar. At around noon on June 25, 1876, the attack of Lt. Gen. George Armstrong Custer's Seventh Cavalry took them by surprise. Suddenly, "the squaws were like flying birds," recalled Sitting Bull, leader of the Hunkpapa: "the bullets were like humming bees."

The women, it turned out, thought of seeking sanctuary first. By dusk, the women and children were moving camp, and by morning they had crossed Greasy Grass Creek, beyond the sound of gunfire, where groups of warriors began to join them. Their annihilation of Custer's forces that day and the next is the most famous defeat of the U.S. army in the history of the West. It is the most famous Indian military victory. It was also, for the remaining Plains tribes, the beginning of the end of freedom. "We kept moving all summer," a man named Red Horse recalled, "the troops being always after us" (Graham 1995, 54–55, 86, 70, 104; Neihardt 1961, 108–9; Hardorff 1991, 92–95).

The Indians had seen this coming. The Sioux and the United States were both expanding their territories, the Sioux ever since many of them left the Great Lakes region for the plains in the late eighteenth century, and the United States in its relentless westward migration that poured across and onto the western plains beginning in the 1840s. They fought bloody battles throughout the 1850s and 1860s and made treaties – at Fort Laramie on the North Platte River in 1851 to control intertribal warfare and protect westering whites, and in 1868 to create a "Great Sioux Reservation" out of what later became South Dakota, with added hunting grounds west in the Yellowstone and Powder River country of present-day Montana and Wyoming. At the same time, in 1869 the Grant administration formed an idealistic Indian Peace Commission just as determined to turn the Plains Indians into crop-growing Christians as the U.S. Army was to round them up or kill them. Even in the 1870s, many Indians disregarded the treaties entirely, especially the young hot-headed ones and those most resistant to change. The Sioux still pushed westward, gaining turf from the Crow. Faced with a choice of falling into the hands of earnest humanitarians or fighting and starving, many chose the latter (Utley 1993, 43, 82; Prucha 1985, 17–21; Greene 1991, 4–5).

By the time Custer and the Seventh Cavalry arrived at the Greasy Grass, the Sioux were restive. In the summer of 1874, Custer himself had led an expedition of soldiers and miners into *Paha Sapa*, the Black Hills, which jut four thousand feet from the plains in what was then the western third of the Great Sioux Reservation, and they found substantial gold deposits there. "From the grass roots down it was 'pay dirt,'" announced the *Chicago Inter-Ocean* newspaper. White fortune seekers, fuelled by the depression of 1873, defied treaty provisions, and the Sioux's young men, who regarded the hills as their reliable "food pack" or storehouse, "began to talk bad," as Sitting Bull put it, against the invaders (Greene 1991, 5; Graham 1995, 68; Utley 1993).

Farther west, Sitting Bull was still preoccupied with fighting the Crow. The government sent commissioners to buy the Black Hills and he refused to even meet with them, scorning other Sioux leaders who considered signing the agreement. Now the whites were infuriated. Fifteen thousand miners already in the Black Hills would not be denied. In December 1875, Grant's Commissioner of Indian Affairs sent the free-roaming bands an ultimatum: report to an agency by January 31, 1876, or face all-out war. "They wanted to give little and get much," noted Sitting Bull (Utley 1993, 116, 126–28, 131; Graham 1995, 68).

The Battle of the Greasy Grass at the end of June, known to whites as the Battle of the Little Big Horn, was actually no contest. The Indians were still elated over a successful attack against Gen. George Crook's forces on Rosebud Creek a week earlier, and although the cavalry had the element of surprise ("We thought we were whipped," Sitting Bull would later say), the Indian warriors outnumbered the soldiers three to one. The Indians fought "without discipline," said Kill Eagle, "like bees swarming out of a hive," and others recalled later that the dust and smoke reminded them of hell. They remembered that the soldiers fought like "a thousand devils" and were "brave and fearless," and that Sitting Bull never even saw Custer. In battle, they said, "Indians and whites were so mixed up that you could hardly tell anything," like "thousands of dogs might look if all of them were mixed together in a fight," covered with white dust, and that in the confusion they killed and scalped one another by mistake. Nevertheless, just as Sitting Bull had foreseen in a vision, the "soldiers without ears" fell "upside-down into camp." None in Custer's immediate command survived. Black Elk, though sickened by the smell of blood, declared himself "a happy boy," but Chief Red Horse, who was digging turnips with the women when the attack began, said, "I don't like to talk about that fight. If I hear any of my people talking about it, I always move away" (Graham 1995, 54, 70, 78, 75, 103; Marquis 1931, 237; Neihardt 1961, 131; Frazier 1989, 180).

As shocked Americans absorbed the defeat that all but spoiled the nation's hundredth anniversary, the Civil War command of Sheridan and Sherman that now directed the War for the West quickly reinforced Gen. George Crook, Gen. Alfred H. Terry, and Col. John Gibbon, who had the Sioux at their backs. To salvage a mission that had quickly turned into a disaster, they sent Lt. Col. Elwell S. Otis and the Twenty-second Infantry to the Dakota Territory, and Col. Nelson Miles and the Fifth Infantry, celebrated Indian fighters in Texas, to the Yellowstone River. Custer, the undisciplined and charismatic soldier, icon of the irrepressible, brazen American, remained so even now. He became the *cause célèbre* that forced the Indians over the medicine line (Greene 1991, 1–4; Utley 1993, 165).

Others, too, would seek sanctuary on the border. Like the Sioux, Canadian Métis and American Nez Percé fled their homelands to cross it between 1877 and 1885. Usually their stories are told separately, as those of distinctive cultures battling separate nations. The Métis, particularly, are commonly presented as the peculiarly Canadian historical sore point of the prairie West. Yet these natives in varying degrees knew one other, conferred about their prospects as they criss-crossed the border, befriended and fought the same white traders and soldiers, and even sought refuge with one another. The medicine line was the thread that bound them together.

Sitting Bull travelled the Sioux country in 1876, unwilling to join those Indians who had started to drift back to their agencies as soon as the wild plums began to ripen, intending instead to winter with his band in their hunting grounds along the Yellowstone and perhaps head north to Canada in the spring. Miles, Crook, and Terry chased them relentlessly. Unlike Crazy Horse, many Sioux were weary of fighting, and said so. Sitting Bull and several leaders of other bands met in a few days in his tepee and agreed to listen to what the soldiers had to say. On October 20, two emissaries met with Miles and arranged a conference for later that day. Sitting Bull and Nelson Miles would come together for the first time at Cedar Creek near the Yellowstone River in east-central Montana Territory (Greene 1991, 66, 88, 89; Campbell n.d.).

The atmosphere was tense. Two hundred mounted warriors stood on a hill a short distance behind the conferees. Miles's troops stood facing the warriors a short distance back, with cannon placed on another hilltop. The meeting soon resembled a game of chicken. The distant soldiers, whom a white observer described as "fidgety," were creeping outward, as if trying to surround the council. Sitting Bull ordered his warriors to do likewise. Miles asked Sitting Bull to order his men to bunch up. The chief said Miles should order his own men to bunch up first. Miles gave the order, Sitting Bull followed suit. After more volleying of challenges and plans in this way, they seemed to agree to a stalemate. They resolved nothing but parted amicably.

When they met again the next day, however, like two gamecocks in a curious dance, their initial politeness had vanished. Tempers flared. In his autobiography, Miles claimed it was Sitting Bull who became enraged. Indian sources claimed that it was Miles who had a belligerent attitude at the second meeting and lost his temper. "You are losing your temper," Sitting Bull said to the Colonel. "Let us dismiss the council."

When the meeting ended, the Indians lit fire to the prairie, which they often did when annoyed. The soldiers, their "strong hearts [growing] weak as our thoughts flew back to the Custer massacre," as trumpeter Edwin M. Brown described it, retaliated with artillery. Casualties totalled two soldiers and perhaps five Sioux. But more importantly for the army's cause, some Sioux from the Minniconjou and Sans Arc bands agreed to make peace with Miles. The Indians' motivations seemed clear. After signing the paper, a leader named Bull Ghost voiced what many of the Indians might have been thinking: "We have now agreed; when do we eat?"

Along with Crazy Horse and the Ogalalas farther south, Sitting Bull, Gall, and the other Hunkpapa continued to hunt for their food. Temperatures plummeted. Miles found the cold "simply appalling." By November it was often ten degrees below zero, and by December, thirty below, with a bitter wind. Miles, his men swaddled in heavy buffalo shoes and overcoats, continued to chase the Indians. After one attack, eleven Cheyenne babies froze in their mothers' arms. At another point during the winter, Miles's lieutenant, Frank Baldwin, found a little howitzer tube and some solid shot at nearby Fort

Peck. He used it to drive Sitting Bull's followers from their camp and managed to seize several hundred buffalo robes, tons of dried meat, and many of their animals. In mid-March, a sudden flood of the Missouri River washed away most of what Sitting Bull's camp had left. The time of reckoning had come. The first week of May 1877, while Crazy Horse and 889 Sioux surrendered at Camp Robinson, Nebraska, Sitting Bull and about a thousand destitute Sioux from some twenty different bands crossed the medicine line into present-day southern Saskatchewan, then part of the huge North-West Territories. "They are hunting me," Sitting Bull lamented, "like wild animals seeking for my blood" (Greene 1991, 120, 129; Utley 1993, 174–75, 179).

Nelson A. Miles was reason enough for the Sioux to flee to Canada – relentless, ambitious, a brilliant field tactician, even though, like many Americans, he cherished the notion of the noble savage even as he chased them down. But Sitting Bull himself was pushing these Sioux. What Custer was to the Sioux War, Sitting Bull became to the medicine line. He turned it into a media event (Miles 1896; Miles 1911; Johnson 1962, 128–29; Utley 1973).

The Battle of the Little Big Horn gave Sitting Bull great notoriety, and in 1877 Sitting Bull was the one the journalists wanted to see. Reporters came to the medicine line to meet the famous Sioux, Custer's nemesis, "the most mysterious Indian chieftain who ever flourished in North America," the one they told their readers held "the magic sway of a Mohammed over the rude war tribes that engirdle him." They sat across from him, enchanted by his charisma, rapt with his expression of "exquisite irony," admiring of his small but powerful hands. Was he the belligerent, conceited, and narrow-minded enemy of white progress? Was he a flexible, politically savvy leader? Since Sitting Bull himself wrote only a hieroglyphic autobiography – a few dozen simple figure drawings recording his exploits as a warrior – his qualities as leader and a borderland strategist take shape in a cloudy tableau of second-hand portraits. He was one among many Sioux head-men, not always the most powerful. Indians respected him, as a warrior, as a spiritual man of inspiring character and wisdom, and as a leader of several elite men's societies, including one he founded called the White Horse Riders. "He had a big brain and a good one," said Wooden Leg, "a strong heart and a generous one" (Finerty 1890; Stirling 1938; Marquis 1931, 383).

Among white Americans he first became known as the determined patriot, as uncompromising as the Ogalala Sioux leader Red Cloud was willing to negotiate. Early writers portrayed Sitting Bull variously as intelligent and principled, a canny savage, pompous, vain, and boastful, and obstinate and belligerent with whites. Later writers gave us a gilded heroism of great Sioux warriors, saintly victims of white genocide. Historian Robert Utley wrote of Sitting Bull as a wise if weary leader, who with growing despondency faced the end of native nomadic life (Anonymous 1891; Johnson 1962; Stillson and Diehl 1877; McGlaughlin 1883, 48–49; Vestal 1934; Utley 1993).

While such portraits have their merits, none fully convey the give-and-take along the borderland. Power still hung in the balance. Before Sitting Bull became the clearly unhappy man of July 20, 1881, when he surrendered his pony and gun to U.S. agents at Fort Buford, he spent several years as a strategist and negotiator, trying to improve his people's position in the complex political landscape of the medicine line. Even in North West Mounted Police Inspector James Morrow Walsh's self-congratulatory memoirs can be found a depiction of Sitting Bull as an intelligent, independent tactician and negotiator, trying to take full advantage of his situation. First, Walsh described the powerful aura of the man, what Walsh called "the love of free life that exists around Bull," which the Sioux leader used to arouse his forces. Sitting Bull's "unsettled camps keep up a constant friction amongst the Indians on both sides of the line," Walsh reported. Moreover, Walsh acknowledged that Sitting Bull had thoughtful, well-developed attitudes and plans for his situation. If he eventually became tractable to the Americans, it was not without a long and deliberate process of negotiation. "Permit me to explain how the change in this man and his followers was brought about," explained Walsh in a report written seven months before Sitting Bull's surrender. "Sitting Bull is the shrewdest and most intelligent Indian living," Walsh wrote. He "has the ambition of Napoleon and is brave to a fault; he is respected as well as feared by every Indian on the plains. In war he has no equal, in council he is superior to all. Every word said by him carries weight, is quoted and passed from camp to camp." In his own tale, Walsh was still the hero, but here also was Sitting Bull's painstaking diplomacy, hardly the kind of protracted debate a "Mephistophelian" savage would demand. "Neither hunger nor prospective starvation in his camp at any time tended to effect it, as many persons imagine, but it was done by patient, hard work, days and nights of steady persuasion, argument, and illustration" (Walsh 1890).

By 1878, buffalo and food were scarce. The Canadian government gave the Sioux ammunition for hunting, but no food, and the credit and goodwill of traders had nearly reached its limit. The Indians had just broken their camp farther east at Wood Mountain and scattered west across the country north of Fort Walsh, determined, as Sitting Bull had once vowed, "[to] send children to hunt and live on prairie mice" rather than surrender to become wards of the United States government.

In the diplomatic triangle that enclosed the United States, Canada, and the Sioux, Sitting Bull did not hesitate to use his keen sense of theatre on his people's behalf. A timeline of Sitting Bull's four years in Canada reads like a diplomat's wartime date book: frequent councils with RCMP officers (particularly Walsh, his favourite); ongoing negotiations with his own followers and hot-headed young warriors, who occasionally required discipline; a reluctant council with the diplomatic envoy of Americans headed by General Terry (where Siting Bull refused to shake hands, and after a long pause and much pipe smoking, delivered a stinging rebuke); and several encounters or attempted alliances with the half-dozen or more groups who had previously found the Sioux less than friendly, including the Nez Percé and two long-standing Sioux enemies, the Crow and the Blackfoot. By 1881, when these native alliances had come to nothing, Walsh's successor, Insp. Lief Crozier, anticipated open warfare between the Sioux and the Canadian Indians. "[They] say they will kill Sitting Bull if they have a chance," he noted. It was a complex borderland, demanding skill in both diplomacy and warfare. Starvation was not the only reason Sitting Bull would cross the medicine line out of Canada for the last time in 1881 (Crozier 1881; Walsh n.d.; Anonymous n.d.; NWMP annual reports 1877–81; Utley 1993, 373, n. 22).

Despite the Indians' long odds, the Sioux thought Sitting Bull was a crackerjack negotiator. A Miniconjou Sioux once dispatched a two-page pictograph to the Cheyenne River Agency to inform agency Indians of their kinfolk's situation in Canada. In reality a political cartoon, it shows General Terry, after negotiations with Sitting Bull and his Sioux delegation, about to shoot himself and fall into a newly dug grave (Hoyt 1877; Anderson 1955).

Under the Indian Act of 1876, a consolidation of laws that has no parallel in the United States, the Canadian government's goals were essentially the same as those of the United States: to protect and control Indian reserves and virtually all aspects of Indian life, and to advance Indian assimilation through the ownership of private property, the practice of agriculture, sobriety, and the franchise – to "train them for a more civilized life," as a member of the House of Commons put it. The Canadian enforcement of this policy through the Mounted Police and the Department of Indian Affairs had its good and bad points. Its officials were less corrupt than those of the U.S. Bureau of Indian Affairs, more gradual in implementing their goals, clearer in their definition of who was Indian. With less settlement pressure than in the United States, they were also afforded the comparative luxury of more time and space (Samek 1987, 19; Thomas 1975, 85–88; Walsh n.d.). "Our actions should be persuasive, not compulsory," wrote a superior to Mountie James Walsh about the Sioux in 1877 (Walsh n.d.). They were also at times neglectful of their wards through inertia, conservatism, or deliberate action. If only the United States could "be moved to prevent further measures of intimidation" against Sitting Bull and his band, observed the governor general of the North-West Territories in 1881, he could "leav[e] hunger to do the work" (Winton 1881).

Sitting Bull's description of Canada as the benevolent "white mother" and the United States as the evil "white father" was a simple and lasting scheme. The story of the Sioux's hegira to the north is still used to illustrate the Canadian government's relatively amicable relationship with native groups, in contrast to the U.S. "reservation or extermination" policy of the late-nineteenth-century plains Indian wars. Sitting Bull's descriptions of national character still apply to the broader and commonly held stereotypes of the two societies: the gentle Canadian mosaic, a loose and sparsely populated allegiance of groups that tolerates differences, versus the violent and rapidly expanding American melting pot that demands assimilation. The North West Mounted Police have long been the symbol of the benevolent authority of the Canadian frontier, just as the United States Army and the Texas Rangers have more recently served as symbols for a brutal, racist white conquest of the American West.

Yet this dichotomy did not portray the situation in which Sitting Bull found himself in the late 1870s. The early northern plains borderland defied simple categories. All sides were engaged in some degree of diplomatic posturing and triangulation – the Americans pretending to want the Sioux back (except for Nelson Miles, anxious to pursue his quarry across the border), but actually happy to unload them onto the Canadians; the Canadians gingerly urging the Sioux to return south while trying not to rile them or appear too sympathetic with the Americans; and the Sioux working whatever advantage they could by using their position on the medicine line to enhance their negotiations and obtain food. Trans-border Blackfoot, Crow, Métis, Sioux, Nez Percé and others flirted with various hostilities and alliances. National differences on the early borderland were more the ambiguous product of circumstances than the absolute character traits of distinct political and cultural traditions (Manzione 1991, 6–18; Pennanen 1970).

RIEL, THE MÉTIS, AND THE BORDER

The Métis, as much as the Sioux, were the quintessential product of circumstances, a kind of cultural, economic, and geographical third rail in Canadian politics – Catholic and mystical; interpreters, guides, and hide and pemmican traders; and a border-straddling community with settlements in Minnesota, Manitoba, and the Montana, Dakota, and North-West Territories. Seven years before the Battle of the Greasy Grass, even before the surveyors had stretched their chains across the prairie, the Métis discovered the power of the border.

On a rainy August morning in 1870, a schoolteacher named James Stewart came galloping through the gates of the Red River settlement's Fort Garry (not yet Winnipeg), found the young Métis leader Louis Riel at his breakfast and gasped, "For the love of God, save yourself." One year after he had run surveyors off of Métis land, the young and charismatic Riel found himself seeking exile as well. The newly formed Canada had just bought the vast western territory of Rupert's Land from the Hudson's Bay Company, including the Red River Métis colony. In the winter of 1869–70, some twelve thousand Métis resisted the sale, delaying the transfer of land with their demands: bilingual institutions, confessional schools, local control of public lands, and provincial status. As leader of the Red River Resistance, Riel allowed a firing squad to execute a white Ontarian named Thomas Scott who opposed him, won most of his demands in the Manitoba Act of 1870 – Métis "language" (French), "religion" (Catholic), and "rights" (to use the land in keeping with their Aboriginal title) – and became the chief target of English Protestant Ontario's wrath against French Catholic Quebec. On that rainy August morning, some of them planned on killing him. For the Métis, as for Riel, the meaning of the border they had ignored for so long was about to become simple: the American side meant sanctuary in exile, the Canadian, persecution or difficulty (McClean 1987; Flanagan 1996, 33–35; Flanagan 2000, 9).

Riel fled across the border. The next fourteen years were spent among a wide network of Métis and Franco-Americans. He stayed with his former Latin teacher in Dakota Territory and briefly in St. Paul, both places he had lived in the 1860s while in his early twenties. (Born in 1844, Riel was about ten years younger than Sitting Bull.) Restless and largely unhappy, he spent brief periods in Manitoba and Quebec evading arrest, and floated among French Canadian homes in New England and New York state; he bargained with Prime Minister Macdonald expecting an official pardon (which never came) for his role in the Resistance; and he visited a Franco-American named Edmund Mallet in Washington, D.C. (Flanagan 2000, 46–49, 54).

In December 1874, the Canadian House of Commons granted Riel amnesty if he agreed to two years' imprisonment or five years' exile from Canada. He chose exile. Within a few months, in an interview with President Grant arranged by Mallet, he presented a plan for a quasi-independent Manitoba, and then had a divine messianic revelation in a Washington, D.C., church. "God," he later wrote, "anointed him [Riel] with His divine gifts and the fruits of His Spirit, as Prophet of the New World." Frustrated in politics and harbouring a case of messianic zeal that even his friends could not distinguish from madness, Riel spent 1876 and 1877 in two suburban Montreal insane asylums. The truth of his mental state has never been finally determined, but once released, he was, ironically, offered a job helping a Catholic missionary to entice Sitting Bull's Sioux back across the border to the United States (Flanagan 2000, 56, 58, 63).

Riel rejected the offer. He had his own divine plan to execute. In December 1878, he wrote a poem saying he would go to fetch the "*nations sauvages*" on the banks of the Missouri to help the Métis. Eight months later he was in an ox cart passing through medicine line country, joining the "Métis hunters of the Big Bend of Milk River" and eating buffalo meat. "I am glad to see the prairie," he wrote home to his mother. Like Sitting Bull and his followers from the

United States trying to become Canadians, Canadian native Riel also thought "it better to begin a career on the other side of the line." ("*I Louis Riel*," he vowed in the Third Judicial District of the Territory of Montana in the spring of 1880, "do declare on oath that it is bona fide my intention to become A Citizen of the United States of America, and to renounce forever all allegiance and fidelity to all and any foreign Prince, Potentate, State and Sovereignty whatsoever, and particularly to *Victoria Queen, of Great Britain and Ireland and Empress of India of whom I am a subject.*")

From 1878 to 1880, while Sitting Bull's Sioux lived just north of the line, criss-crossing it to hunt buffalo, Riel and Métis "in force" lived just south of the line on the Milk River doing the same. Riel's whole design, though, was to over-come the border. He believed that the Métis and Indians held Aboriginal title, not of use but of ownership, to western lands. He dreamed of a great confed-eracy of native peoples, which, under the circumstances, was not so far-fetched. Others had already made overtures for tribal alliances: the Cree chief Big Bear to the Blackfeet and Sioux in the Cypress Hills area; Sitting Bull to the Cheyenne before the Battle of the Greasy Grass, and in Canada to the Blackfoot leader Crowfoot (for whom Sitting Bull named his son). Riel envisioned a pan-native alliance, using Montana as a base to invade Canada and create an independent native republic, setting himself up as a New World Prophet (Flanagan 2000, 111, 113–15; Riel 1985, 218–19, 220n4, 220–21, 221n1).

Riel became a trader, shepherd, ranch hand, and teacher. He spent time at Forts Assiniboine and Belknap, married a Métis hunter's daughter named Marguerite Monet, and eventually moved to nearby Carroll on the Missouri River, a place the Helena (Montana) *Daily Herald* described as a small hamlet "in a barren, cheerless country" with a population of eighteen. Like a labour organizer, he worked to unite the many native factions, apparently without mentioning his mission's religious significance. In the summer of 1879 he signed an agreement in blood (or red ink) with the Assiniboine declaring that the country belonged to "the Indians and their brothers the half-breeds." In December, Crowfoot and his Blackfoot went south of the line to join Riel's Métis for the winter, about when Riel also appealed to Chief Big Bear and the Cree. In January, Sitting Bull came south of the line to meet with the Métis leader. In August 1880, Riel made an offer to Gen. Nelson Miles to use his influence among the Indians in exchange for a Métis reservation. Riel was a compelling figure and a great orator, but for reasons we shall never really know, the others rejected his appeals (Riel 1985, 246n2; Flanagan 2000, 116–18, 120, 122).

The Métis, however, still looked to him for leadership. In the winter of 1885, the discontent in the central North-West Territories (now central Saskatchewan) was palpable. The Métis, nearly buffalo-less as the last of the herds were killed, and with their transportation services threatened by steamboats and railroads, had lost the basis of their economy. They wanted land, either grants for what they had already settled along the South Saskatchewan River or scrip – a certificate for all Métis heads-of-family redeemable for Dominion lands – that they could sell to land speculators, as they had done after the Manitoba Act of 1870. The Indians, also without buffalo or a livelihood, had little recourse but to seek rations on reservations. The Canadian whites, both farmers and businessmen led by a young man from the town of Prince Albert named William Henry Jackson, were infuriated by distant control over their services, transportation, taxes, tariffs, and their lives generally. They wanted provincial status and greater local control, and they even threatened secession.

Rebellion, at least according to many Métis, required Louis Riel. He was, in Machiavelli's phrase, their "prophet in arms." In June 1884, a contingent of four rode down across the border to Montana to get him. By then Riel had become a schoolteacher of Blackfeet children at St. Peter's Mission in Carroll, where he spent his evenings writing passionate verse on religion and politics in a cabin whose poverty surprised his visitors. Here was their hero, humbly devoted to a calling, but required by higher purpose. They could not have appealed more to Riel's messianic sense of mystical significance. "The whole race is calling for you," they wrote in a letter they presented to him in the mission yard, where they had called him out of mass. Making the most of the occasion, he wrote out his response, which he gave them the next day: "[Y]our personal visit does me honor and causes me great pleasure.... I record it as one of the gratifications of my life" (McClean 1987, 164–65; Howard 1952; Riel 1985, 220n4).

When he passed through medicine line country into central Saskatchewan just north of the town of Battleford, Riel discovered that an alliance would require various forms of persuasion. With the Indians, he tried histrionics. Blackfoot leader Crowfoot recalled that Riel publicly trampled on a copy of

Treaty No. 6 (one of several treaties the Canadian government made in the 1870s to place natives on reserves), in an effort to convince the Blackfoot "to join with all the Sioux, and Crees, and half-breeds ... [to] capture the North-West, and hold it for the Indian race and the Métis." With whites, Riel met with William Henry Jackson and gave moderate, reasonable-sounding speeches, although Jackson and his followers disagreed immovably that the Métis had claim to Aboriginal rights. Once again facing many irreconcilable groups, Riel failed to persuade. By March 1885, he managed to assemble a paltry force of a few hundred men – Métis and a few Saulteaux, Cree, Sioux, and Canadian allies – into a last gasp of native armed resistance against the Canadian government. "We march, my braves!" Riel cried as he proclaimed the Provisional Government of Saskatchewan. At every halt in their progress against better-armed Mounties and Canadian militia, Louis Riel made his motley rebels recite the rosary. The rebellion lasted eight weeks – from March 18 to May 12, 1885. The Canadian government fielded about eight thousand Mounties and volunteers, its first national army, which won by sheer force of numbers. Even the Blackfoot, inspired by food and ammunition, fought on the government's side. By November 16, Riel had been captured, tried, convicted of treason, and hung (Beal and Macleod 1984, 67–68; McClean 1896, 380; Flanagan 2000, 100).

Years before, in 1879, a group of Métis arrested in Montana Territory had been asked their nationality. Ten said they were British, and were escorted to Canada; 140 said they were American, and were advised to settle on the high plains of central Montana. We do not know why they responded this way. But judging from native leaders, the medicine line was a temporary expedient. Sitting Bull remained emphatically Sioux. Riel, nominally a citizen of the United States, remained a Métis at heart. "It sored my heart to say that kind of adieu," Riel later mourned publicly of his new citizenship, "to my mother, to my brothers, to my sisters, to my friends, to my countrymen, my native land" (Dewdney 1880).

When Riel crossed the medicine line for the last time in mid-June of 1884, loaded with his wife, two children, and few possessions in a Red River cart, he marked the end of an era. With Riel died the natives' hope of crossing to safety or a better life – of returning to the native geography not just of one's homeland but of the heart. Except for the Ghost Dance religion of 1890, the desperate set of skirmishes known as the Riel Rebellion was the last great attempt at native unity along the medicine line in the nineteenth century (Friesen 1984, 227).

CHIEF JOSEPH, THE NEZ PERCÉ, AND THE BORDER

History loves a dramatic failure. On a frigid September 30, 1877, on the grassy plain halfway between the badland "breaks" of the Missouri river and the shallow trough of the Milk River just south of the U.S.-Canada border, the Nez Percé surrendered to U.S. soldiers at the Battle of the Bear Paws. They had fled for 115 days, over a thousand miles in a long, winding route through southern Montana from their eastern Oregon and Idaho homeland – their sad journey a kind of northern version of the Cherokee Trail of Tears – to escape the gold seekers, settlers, and bad treaties forcing them out of their ancestral homeland in Wallowa valley onto a smaller reservation. A refined, honest, friendly people whose livelihood depended on salmon, buffalo, and their Appaloosa herds, they endured many deaths and grim prospects and when all that remained was one final dash across the border to sanctuary, Gen. Nelson A. Miles took them by surprise. After all that, they were caught in a web laid for the Sioux.

The Nez Percé were taken prisoner and sent to Fort Leavenworth, Kansas, where many died, and on to Indian Territory. The battle is remembered in popular history by the words attributed to Chief Joseph at the formal surrender, when the sun "was dropping to the level of the prairie and tinging the tawny and white land with waves of ruddy lights." "Hear me, my chiefs," said Joseph in the fading light; "I am tired; my heart is sick and sad. From where the sun now stands, I will fight no more forever." The popular legend deflated, however, when the original pencil draft of the report was revealed to show the handwriting of the later poet and lawyer Lt. C. E. S. Wood who claimed to have taken down the great chief's words on the spot. In the margin it read, "Here insert Joseph's reply to the demand for surrender" (Walsh n.d.; Brown 1967, 407–8, 428).

The battlefield ten miles south of Chinook is little changed from the way it looked in 1877. You can read the revisionist Park Service plaque describing "the usual forked tongue methods of the whites, which had deprived these

Indians of their hereditary lands," and the trails through the prairie battlefield cast an eerie peacefulness over the scene. Tiny red, yellow, white, and blue medicine bundles, tied together like kite tails with white string, rest next to cylindrical silver markers about the size of automatic sprinkler heads imprinted with the names of famous Nez Percé. Looking Glass, the formidable military brains of the Nez Percé's flight from Idaho, had the top of his head shot off on a little hillock. Too-hool-hool-zote, another leader remembered for his thick, powerful build and deep-voiced resistance, died nearby in a rifle pit. So did Chief Joseph's brother, Ollicut. Even more than the Sioux or the Métis, the Nez Percé felt the limits of law along the medicine line.

After their surrender, a few hundred Nez Percé managed to slip into Canada and temporary asylum – "some riding double and crying," as one Sioux remembered – carrying wounded children into the Sioux's Canadian camps across the line. Though the Nez Percé were long-standing enemies in a harsh political climate, the outraged Sioux took them in as brothers, "all packed like sardines," the Sioux witness remembered, in too few tepees. The village of hope, they all were learning, was rapidly running out of room (Campbell n.d.; Turner 1950, 342).

NOTE

1   Some of this material appears in slightly different form in Beth LaDow's *The Medicine Line.*

SOURCES

Anderson, Harry H. 1955. "A Sioux Pictorial Account of General Terry's Council at Fort Walsh, October 17, 1877." *North Dakota History* 27.

Anonymous, Indian Affairs. n.d. Records and correspondence regarding Sitting Bull and the American Sioux, microfilm. Public Archives of Canada, RG 10, Vol. 3691, File 13, 893, and RG 19, Vol. 3652, File 8589, Pt. 1.

Anonymous. "The Story of Sitting Bull: Was He A Winnipegger?" Newspaper clipping, January 3, 1891. n.p. Public Archives of Canada, Indian Affairs, RG 10, Vol. 3691, File 13, 893.

Beal, Bob and Rod Macleod. 1984. *Prairie Fire: The 1885 North-West Rebellion.* Edmonton: Hurtig.

Brown, Mark M. 1967. *The Flight of the Nez Perce.* Lincoln: University of Nebraska Press.

Cameron, Elspeth. 1997. *Canadian Culture: An Introductory Reader.* Toronto: Canadian Scholars' Press.

Campbell Walter Stanley. Collection. n.d. "Old Bull Tells ... ," Box 105, notebook 11. Division of Manuscripts, Western History Collection, Univ. of Oklahoma Libraries.

Crozier, Leif N. F. Letter to Dep. Minister of the Interior, May 3, 1880. Public Archives of Canada, Department of Indian Affairs, RG 10, Vol. 3652, File 8589, Pt. 1.

_____. Letter to Lieutenant Colonel Dennis, May 3, 1881. Public Archives of Canada, Indian Affairs microfilm, RG 10, Vol. 3652, File 8589, Pt. 1.

Dewdney, Edgar. Letter from Indian Commissioner to Commissioner of Indian Affairs, North-West Territories, January 2, 1889. Canada Sessional Papers No. 4, 1880, Pt. 1, Report of the Deputy Superintendent-General of Indian Affairs, 1879, 88.

Finerty, John Frederick. 1890. *War-path and Bivouac, or the Conquest of the Sioux, a Narrative of Stirring Personal Experiences and Adventures in the Big Horn and Yellowstone Expedition of 1876, and in the Campaign on the British Border, in 1879.* Chicago: M. A. Donohue.

Flanagan, Thomas. 2000. *Riel and the Rebellion: 1885 Reconsidered,* 2d ed. Toronto: University of Toronto Press.

_____. 1996. *Louis "David" Riel: Prophet of the New World,* rev. ed. Toronto: University of Toronto Press.

Frazier, Ian. 1989. *Great Plains.* New York: Farrar, Straus, Giroux.

Friesen, Gerald. 1984. *The Canadian Prairies: A History*. Lincoln: University of Nebraska Press.

Graham, W. A. ed. 1995. *The Custer Myth: A Source Book of Custeriana*. Mechanicsburg, PA: Stackpole Books. (Originally published 1953.)

Greene, Jerome A. 1991. *Yellowstone Command: Colonel Nelson A. Miles and the Great Sioux War, 1876–1877*. Lincoln: University of Nebraska Press.

Hardorff, Richard G., comp. and ed. 1991. *Lakota Recollections of the Custer Fight: New Sources of Indian Military History*. Lincoln: University of Nebraska Press.

Higheagle, Robert. Manuscript. n.d. Walter Stanley Campbell Collection, University of Oklahoma, box 104, folder 21, 41.

Howard, Joseph Kinsey. 1952. *Strange Empire: A Narrative of the Northwest*. New York: Morrow.

Hoyt, Lt. R. M. Letter to Post Adjutant, Cheyenne River Agency, November 20, 1877. (U.S.) Bureau of Indian Affairs, RG 74, National Archives and Records Administration, M234, Roll 130, Frame 418.

Irvine, Acheson G. 1877. North-West Mounted Police Annual Report.

Johnson, Virginia W. 1962. *The Unregimented General: A Biography of Nelson A. Miles*. Cambridge, MA: The Riverside Press, Houghton Mifflin Company.

Manzione, Joseph. 1991. *I am Looking to the North for My Life': Sitting Bull, 1876–1881*. Salt Lake City: University of Utah Press.

Marquis, Thomas B. 1931. *Wooden Leg, a Warrior Who Fought Custer*. Lincoln: University of Nebraska Press.

McClean, Donald George. 1987. *Home From the Hill : A History of the Métis in Western Canada*. Regina: Gabriel Dumont Institute of Native Studies and Applied Research.

McClean, John. 1896. *Canadian Savage Folk*. Toronto: William Briggs.

McGlaughlin, James. Annual report, Commissioner of Indian Affairs, August 15, 1883.

Miles, Nelson A. 1896. *Personal Recollections and Observations of General Nelson A. Miles*. Chicago: The Werner Company.

_____. 1911. *Serving the Republic: Memoirs of the Civil and Military Life of Nelson A. Miles, Lieutenant-General, United States Army*. New York: Harper & Brothers.

Neihardt, John G. 1961. *Black Elk Speaks: Being the Life Story of a Holy Man of the Oglala Sioux*. Lincoln: University of Nebraska Press.

Pennanen, Gary. 1970. "Sitting Bull: Indian Without a Country." *Canadian Historical Review*, June, 51, 123–40.

Prucha, Francis Paul. 1985. *The Indians in American Society from the Revolutionary War to the Present*. Berkeley: University of California Press.

Riel, Louis. 1985. *The Collected Writings of Louis Riel*, Vol. 2, gen. ed. George F.G. Stanley. Edmonton: University of Alberta Press.

Samek, Hana. 1987. *The Blackfoot Confederacy, 1880–1920*. Albuquerque: University of New Mexico Press.

Stillson, Jerome and Charles Diehl. 1877. *Chicago Times*, October 22, 23.

Stirling, Mathew W. 1938. *Three Pictographic Autobiographies of Sitting Bull*. Smithsonian Miscellaneous Collections, vol. 97, no. 5. Washington, D.C.: Smithsonian Institution.

Thomas, Lewis G., ed. 1975. *The Prairie West to 1905: A Canadian Sourcebook*. Toronto: Oxford University Press.

Turner, John Peter. 1950. *The North-West Mounted Police, 1873–1893*, vol. 1. Ottawa: E. Cloutier, King's Printer.

Utley, Robert M. 1973. *Frontier Regulars: The United States Army and the Indian, 1866–1890*. New York: Macmillan.

———. 1993. *The Lance and the Shield: The Life and Times of Sitting Bull*. New York: Henry Holt.

Vestal, Stanley. 1934. *Warpath: The True Story of the Fighting Sioux Told in a Biography of Chief White Bull*. Lincoln: University of Nebraska Press.

Walsh, James Morrow. n.d. Walsh Papers. MG6, Public Archives of Manitoba, Winnipeg.

———. Walsh Papers. 1890. "An Account of the Sioux Indians 1976–1879." May. Provincial Archives of Canada, M705, Public Archives of Manitoba, Winnipeg.

Winton, Lieutenant Colonel. 1881. Letter from Secretary to the Governor General, to the Privy Council. February 11. Public Archives of Canada, Indian Affairs, RG 10, vol. 3652, file 8589, pt. 1.

Chapter 5

Disputing the Medicine Line: The Plains Cree and the Canadian-American Border, 1876–85

Michel Hogue, University of Wisconsin-Madison

Just south of the international boundary between Montana and Canada's North-West Territories, on November 7, 1881, Lt. Gustavus Doane and a detachment of the Second U.S. Cavalry arrested Chief Foremost Man (Nekaneet) and seven other Canadian Cree. After confiscating the Crees' guns, knives, and even some of their clothing, soldiers imprisoned the men for several days in a dark cell at Fort Assiniboine before finally releasing them at the border with a warning to stay in Canada or face severe punishment. In harsh November weather, the barefooted men struggled toward Chief Piapot's camp in the Cypress Hills, thirty miles from Fort Walsh. Two died from starvation and exposure en route, though six managed to reach the camp. The Crees' crime: hunting and trading on U.S. soil.[1]

Between 1876 and 1885, the cross-border movement of the Plains Cree, so-called "British Indians" who inhabited the borderlands, drew the attention of officials charged with the administration of Native peoples.[2] Increasingly determined to make the border a meaningful divide and separate "American" Indians from "Canadian" Indians, both governments attempted to restrict the

Crees' movement across the border and remove them from the region. At the same time, faced with dramatic changes to their subsistence patterns, Cree bands showed equal determination to remain in the area to exploit opportunities for hunting, trade, war, and sanctuary.

Although a dominant force on the northern plains by the mid-nineteenth century, the Cree were relatively recent arrivals to the region. Their expansion into the plains stemmed, in part, from the establishment of Hudson's Bay Company fur-trading posts in the lands they traditionally occupied near Hudson Bay and Lake Superior in the seventeenth century. Proximity to the posts gave the Cree preferential access to guns and trade goods that enabled them to act as intermediaries between traders and other tribes. As the fur trade spread west along the Saskatchewan River and its tributaries after the 1760s, the Crees' intermediary role lessened, but they gained new opportunities to supply pemmican and other provisions traders needed to journey to trading companies' new posts in the subarctic. Gradually, a growing number of Cree and their Assiniboine allies from the northern forests and parklands moved onto the plains and adopted a buffalo-hunting lifestyle. At the height of their southward and westward expansion in the 1860s, the Plains Cree ranged throughout most of present-day southern Saskatchewan and east-central Alberta.[3]

The Crees' presence in the region was also closely linked to the expansion of the Assiniboine and Saulteaux (or Plains Ojibwa), with whom some Plains Cree bands travelled, hunted, intermarried, and joined in war against common enemies. After 1840 many Métis buffalo hunters, the offspring of European fur traders and Cree and Ojibwa women, also joined these groups. Their expansion onto the plains displaced Lakota, Crow, and Gros Ventre to the south and the Blackfeet and Sarcee to the west.[4]

As both the number of Cree living on the plains and the commercial demand for hides increased, the great buffalo herds north of the forty-ninth parallel began to shrink. Drawn south by the contraction of these herds and by the high price American traders offered for buffalo robes, the southernmost of the Cree bands established a presence in northern Montana. In 1831–32 the U.S. government granted the Cree a measure of recognition when officials invited Chief Broken Arm (Maskepetoon) and representatives from other tribes living near Fort Union to meet President Andrew Jackson in Washington

D.C. By the 1850s, the Cree-Assiniboine and Western Qu'Appelle people, the southernmost Cree bands, inhabited the borderlands between Wood Mountain and the Cypress Hills and traded at both British posts along the South Saskatchewan River and at American Missouri River posts.[5]

Under increasing hunting pressure, buffalo populations continued to decline, creating a subsistence crisis for tribes on the Canadian prairies by the 1870s. The Cree responded, in part, by pressing the government for treaties as a means to guarantee their survival. In 1874 and 1876 the Cree, Assiniboine, and Ojibwa of central Alberta and southern Saskatchewan concluded Treaties No. 4 and 6 with the Canadian government that, in the government's eyes, extinguished their Aboriginal title to the land. In exchange, the government agreed to supply annual cash payments and agricultural implements and to set aside reserves in consultation with the signatory bands, though the treaties contained no timeline for relocation onto reserves and stipulated that signatory bands could continue to fish and hunt as they had previously done. In some cases, bands that were anxious to make a start in agriculture selected their reserves and had them surveyed by the government in the following year. Others, like Piapot, initially refused to select a reserve even after agreeing to the treaty. Many Plains Cree bands, such as the large camps of Battle River Cree under Chiefs Big Bear and Little Pine, demanded better treaty terms and refused to sign the treaties altogether. These chiefs, among the most influential Cree leaders, remained on the plains with their numerous followers, largely dependent on the hunt.[6]

By 1878 all plains bands faced a severe subsistence crisis, but the Canadian government, despite its treaty promises, made very few provisions for their support, forcing increasing numbers of both treaty and non-treaty Indians to hunt in Montana. In 1879–80 the last remaining buffalo disappeared from Canadian territory.

In Montana, Canadian Indians encountered diverse tribes – the Blackfeet, Crow, Assiniboine, Gros Ventre, Lakota – in competition for the region's resources and facing the U.S. government's growing administrative presence. In the years after the Civil War the federal government set aside the land north of the Missouri River between the Continental Divide and Dakota Territory as territory reserved for resident tribes and established agencies to serve these populations. In accordance with federal Indian policy, agencies on the Teton

River and at Forts Browning, Peck, and, later, Belknap distributed annuities and rations. In return, tribes were expected to engage in agricultural pursuits and generally adopt "civilized" ways. However, since agency provisions were often inadequate, these Indians remained dependent on hunting for food and clothing, and competition for the dwindling game resources intensified.[7]

After 1876, U.S. officials' uneasiness over growing concentrations of diverse tribes was wrapped up in deeper concerns about the presence of Sitting Bull and several thousand refugee Lakota camped just north of the international boundary. The Lakota, anxious to impress on authorities their right to remain in Canada, claimed a long-standing presence north of the forty-ninth parallel and emphasized their historic ties with the British.[8] Although eager to avoid assuming responsibility for the refugees, Canadian officials allowed the Lakota to remain in the North-West Territories under the protection of the Dominion so long as they remained peaceful, but they would receive neither official recognition nor government assistance.

For their part, many Montanans believed the Lakotas' presence just over the border and the threat of prolonging ten years of open warfare discouraged settlement and harmed local business interests. The fighting along the Bozeman Trail and Custer's defeat still fresh in their minds, they clamoured for a string of new military posts along the northern border. The War Department obliged, building Fort Assinniboine near the Bear Paw Mountains in 1879 and Fort Maginnis in the Judith Basin in 1880, ostensibly to guard against "foreign" Indians crossing into the United States and potential disturbances by "American" Indians who left their territory.[9]

By 1879, the growing presence of Indians from north of the border began to alarm American army officials. Reacting to this fear, Col. Thomas Ruger, commander of the District of Montana, declared that although these tribes had long hunted in the region north of the Missouri River, decreasing game populations made it necessary to prohibit hunting parties crossing into Montana from "the other side."[10]

In a response, at once pragmatic and self-serving, Prime Minister John A. Macdonald defended the Canadian policy of allowing tribes to cross the border. He declared it almost impossible for either nation to control the movement of the nomadic tribes. "We might as well try to check the flight of locusts from the South or the rush of buffalo from the North," Macdonald argued.

According to the prime minister, if the United States could not prevent the flight of the Lakota north, it should come as no surprise that Canada could not prevent southward migrations. Adding fuel to the fire, North West Mounted Police Commissioner James F. Macleod asserted that the U.S. Army's manoeuvres prevented the migration of the buffalo into Canadian territory, leaving Indians unable to hunt for their subsistence on either side of the line, and he reminded U.S. officials that it had long been Canada's policy to allow groups of American Peigan, Assiniboine, and Pend d'Oreille to hunt north of the forty-ninth parallel. Macleod urged an agreement that would allow Native peoples in search of food free movement across the border.[11]

The Canadian government could well afford to delay any attempts to confine Indians to reserves. Unlike in the United States, in 1879 the small settler population of the North-West Territories was clustered along the North Saskatchewan and Battle rivers, well north of the forty-ninth parallel, and officials faced little pressure to restrict the cross-border movement of the Cree or other tribes. It served Canada's interests for its Native population to continue hunting in Montana. Indeed, Canadian officials acknowledged the buffalo as their "best allies," and between 1879 and 1881 actively encouraged Indians to go south as a way to reduce the cost of rations.[12]

U.S. authorities, however, resisted allowing Canadian Indians to enter the United States. In summer 1879, the U.S. Army took steps to evict "foreign" Indians in response to Fort Peck agent N. S. Porter's complaint that bands of "hostile Sioux" prevented agency bands from hunting. Under orders from Brig. Gen. Alfred Terry, Col. Nelson A. Miles and his command evicted a large camp of Lakota near Beaver Creek and captured 829 Métis and Indians identified as Canadian, including twenty lodges of non-treaty Cree hunting north of the Milk River. For the remainder of the summer, the army patrolled the territory between Fort Benton and Fort Peck with the intention of expelling Lakota hunting parties and barring all whites, "foreign" Indians, and Métis from hunting in northern Montana.[13]

This action unsettled Canadian authorities, and in negotiations with the United States, the Canadian government in October 1879 secured Secretary of State William Evart's consent to allow "British Indians" to follow the buffalo across the border so long as they did not come with hostile intent or accompanied by "hostile Sioux." This approval was timely, for in his annual report for 1880, Canadian Indian Commissioner Edgar Dewdney estimated that between seven thousand and eight thousand Canadian Indians were living in the Milk River region of Montana. During winter 1880 trader James Willard Schultz reported a large Cree band under Big Bear camped alongside Blackfeet chief Crowfoot and a large group of Métis buffalo hunters, including Louis Riel, near his post at Carroll about a hundred and fifty miles downriver from Fort Benton. Canadian authorities blamed American traders like Schultz for keeping Canadian bands south of the border by offering large sums of money and gifts in exchange for buffalo robes and their treaty annuities.[14]

Although such portrayals fit with perceptions of Indians as influenced by self-interested traders, more complex motives likely prompted cross-border migration. Crossing the border allowed the Cree to obtain goods unavailable on one side of the border or to take advantage of more favourable trade terms. For example, when North West Mounted Police Commissioner Acheson G. Irvine, who replaced Commissioner Macleod in 1880, refused to sell ammunition to Cree bands assembled at Fort Walsh in summer 1882, they informed him they would purchase ammunition at Fort Belknap.[15]

Despite the agreement allowing them to hunt in the United States, the Cree often encountered difficult conditions in the borderlands. Judith Basin buffalo herds, while still large, moved unpredictably, and the Cree who crossed the border were not guaranteed of finding buffalo, especially after 1880. In spring 1880 thousands of starving Indians returned to Canada suffering the effects of a severe winter, scarce food, the loss of hundreds of horses to raiders, and rampant whisky trading in their camps.

Other conflicts arose as American cattlemen, Montana Indians, and Indian agents blamed Canadian tribes for stock losses. In his memoirs, Granville Stuart alleged that bands of Cree and other "British" Indians butchered thousands of head of cattle during winter 1880. Stuart claimed the bands travelled to Montana after receiving their annuity payments in Canada, exchanged their money for whisky, killed cattle, stole horses, and then returned north. Tribes in the United States were often equally displeased with the Canadian Indians. During winter 1880, a group of Assiniboine accompanied by soldiers appeared at Big Bear and Crowfoot's camp, blaming them for the loss of their cattle. "All of you from Canada – Crees, Blackfoot, Sarcees – I count you as one," the chief stated, "I blame you for the loss of our cattle and I want you to give us ten of your best horses as payment." The Assiniboine chief's assertions, whether founded or not, were backed by the force of the U.S. Army.[16]

As they moved back and forth between Canada and the United States, the boundaries that mattered for the Cree were not only the border, but also the boundaries between indigenous groups in the region. The Cree knew that the U.S. government had set aside the area north of the Missouri River for other tribes' use. They therefore sought arrangements with local tribes that would allow them to remain in the territory. Foremost Man and the Cree imprisoned at Fort Assinniboine in November 1881 believed they would be allowed to trade at Fort Belknap since the previous fall Piapot had taken a collection from the Cree camps assembled in the Cypress Hills in order to pay the "chief at Assinaboine" to allow them to hunt and trade. In 1879, Louis Riel apparently made a deal that allowed Métis and Indians to hunt on either side of the international boundary, regardless of nationality. Riel also secured the consent of Colonel Black, the commanding officer at Fort Assinniboine, to allow the Métis to overwinter at the Big Bend of the Milk River.[17]

Indeed, throughout the 1870s various groups of Canadian Indians common-ly received government permission to hunt in northern Montana, and Indian agents' reports indicated that foreign Indians repeatedly visited the agencies in search of relief or to visit relatives. Their presence complicated the creation of agency rolls, and agents often noted the difficulty of sorting out whether Assiniboine and Blackfeet, whom both national governments recognized as belonging within their territories, should be considered American or British, especially as they continued to move back and forth across the border.[18]

By the 1880s, agents demonstrated less tolerance for this mobility. Fort Belknap agent W. L. Lincoln charged that the agency's Gros Ventre, Assiniboine, and Crow all returned to the post after hostile tribes drove them from the hunt. Lincoln thought it time that the large numbers of "half-breeds" and other "British subjects" were "made to remain on their own territory and cease to dominate upon territory belonging to the U.S. and set apart for the Indians of this Agency."[19] The Crees' status as "foreign-ers" marked them as easy targets for exclusion. Agents' counterparts north of the forty-ninth parallel shared the belief that the Plains Crees' treaties with the Canadian government and historic ties to the Hudson's Bay Company established them as "Canadian." The question of where in Canada the Cree belonged, however, remained unsettled.

Between 1879 and 1881 several Cree and Assiniboine bands requested that the Canadian government set aside reserves for them in the vicinity of the Cypress Hills. The Department of Indian Affairs consented. In 1880 it surveyed a reserve for Long Lodge and The Man Who Took the Coat's bands of Assiniboine and planned another for Cowesses's mixed Cree and Saulteaux band. The department established two agency farms near the proposed reserves and in 1880 appointed an Indian agent at Fort Walsh. Other chiefs, Little Pine and Piapot among them, also selected reserves northeast of the fort, although the Department of Indian Affairs never surveyed the proposed reserves. The goal of these leaders, according to historian John Tobias, was to concentrate Native peoples on contiguous reserves in an effort to press their demands for changes to the treaties and preserve a measure of autonomy. By spring 1881, however, officials began to reassess the desirability of allowing concentrations of Cree in the Cypress Hills area.[20]

In spring 1881 thousands of nearly starving Cree who had spent the winter hunting in Montana returned to Fort Walsh to receive their annuity payments and rations. There they met bands of Cree and Assiniboine who had left their reserves along the North Saskatchewan, Battle, and Qu'Appelle rivers to hunt buffalo near the international boundary. Realizing the buffalo were too far south, they chose to remain near Fort Walsh, destitute and largely dependent on rations. Poundmaker, one of the leading Cree chiefs, voiced his complaints that the government had failed to fulfill treaty promises and warned the assembled tribes that if they moved to reserves in the north they would starve. Indian Affairs officials charged that Poundmaker was exciting sedition; they feared that he and Big Bear planned the gathering in order to "wring large inducements from the government" and secure improved treaty terms.[21]

Another incident at Fort Walsh in fall 1880 had likewise illustrated to Canadian officials the difficulties in controlling large gatherings of hungry and discontented people. Dissatisfied with the way the North West Mounted Police had handled a white resident's assault on a member of Lucky Man's band, a group of Cree destroyed the man's vegetable garden. When Agent Edwin Allen informed the culprits that he would deduct the damage from their rations, the situation became tense, and, apparently, only the intervention of Piapot defused it. Officials took note. The following spring Allen received orders to force Cree who arrived at Fort Walsh to move north to their reserves, withhold rations from those who refused, and to do all he could to prevent the Cree from again crossing the border.[22]

Allen had little success in preventing congregations. In late July 1881 over three thousand Indians were drawing rations at Fort Walsh, and officials expected thousands more under Big Bear to arrive from Montana. Instructed to pay treaty annuities only to those who had selected reserves in the Cypress Hills, Inspector of Indian Agencies Thomas P. Wadsworth informed those fleeing northern reserves that they could only receive payments there. The Assiniboine who were settled on the Cypress Hills reserve, however, refused to accept payments until the others from the north received their annuities. The standoff intensified when Lucky Man and Little Pine told Wadsworth they would make him pay "every native of this country" and refused to accept their payments unless the Métis also assembled at the fort were allowed into the treaties. Wadsworth refused their demands and withheld further payments.[23]

The situation became so tense that on August 11 officers confined the North West Mounted Police garrison at Fort Walsh to the barracks, issued each policeman extra Winchester rifles, and ordered seven-pound guns placed in the bastions to cover the sides of the fort's stockade. Only persistent reports of buffalo within twenty miles of Fort Walsh defused the situation. By August 20, Inspector Wadsworth completed the annuity payments to all treaty Indians, including those from the north, and the Cree prepared to leave for the hunt while others returned to their reserves. As the spectacle of the North West Mounted Police garrison confined within the walls of Fort Walsh confirmed, Canadian authorities were in no position to enforce policies the tribes did not like. "The Indians know their strength and when driven by hunger would use it to have their demands satisfied," Wadsworth claimed.[24]

Whereas Canadian officials had earlier encouraged the Crees' migration to Montana, by 1881 they began to look upon such movement with less tolerance. With Canadian Pacific Railway tracks advancing across the prairies, officials anticipated a flood of white settlers into the region. To attract settlers, the government believed it needed to demonstrate that Indians posed no threat or nuisance. Also, so long as Canadian Indians remained near the border, so too did the problem of Natives raiding stock on one side of the border and then skipping across the "medicine line." Given these concerns, Inspector Wadsworth and other officials advocated closing Fort Walsh in order to prevent further congregations and incidents.[25]

As the cattle industry in Montana's Chouteau County and Judith Basin rapidly expanded, clashes between Indians and stockmen increased. In August 1881 the Montana press reported thousands of Canadian Indians returning to northern Montana to hunt. Steeling themselves for the influx, stockmen gathered in Fort Benton to form the Chouteau and Meagher Counties Stock Protective Association. Its members supported Chouteau County Sheriff John J. Healy's plan to "stop the Indians at the line" by organizing a force of fifty armed men to intercept groups bound for the Judith Basin. Warning such collisions could lead to a bloody and expensive war, in September 1881 Montana territorial delegate Martin Maginnis called on the secretary of the interior to confine American Indians to their territory and to prevent "British" Indians from crossing the border. Secretary of the Interior S. J. Kirkwood's response – that under the terms of an October 1855 treaty the Blackfeet and other tribes had the right to leave their territory to hunt – inflamed Granville Stuart and other stockmen. Stuart threatened that stockmen had little choice but to protect their interests.[26]

The prospect of armed parties of stockmen alarmed Brigadier-General Terry, and he voiced his concern about the "serious evils" that would result from the formation of such semimilitary organizations. That fall Colonel Ruger ordered Fort Assiniboine's commanding officer Captain R. L. Morris to compel the "Canadian Indians to here-after remain on their proper side of the boundary line." If they refused to comply, Ruger counselled, troops should use sufficient force to push them back.[27]

Accordingly, a column led by Capt. Jacob Kline began scouting the Milk River country between Fort Belknap and Peoples Creek north of the Little Rocky Mountains on October 8, dispersing camps of Métis and Cree along the way. On October 24, soldiers broke up Piapot's camp of thirty-two lodges. Some army officers remained skeptical of the manoeuvres; Lt. Gustavus Doane stated that "the report about war between Cree halfbreeds and Gros Ventre's – is all nonsense." Doane predicted that the "moment our backs our [sic] turned they will come over again – and go for buffalo – Most of which are now south of Milk River."[28]

Indeed, many Cree remained in the borderlands despite the army's effort. Just as Doane suggested, many returned to Montana shortly after being forced across the border while others avoided the patrols altogether. Indian agent Cecil Denny reported that after the army evicted them from Montana, various chiefs sent runners to Fort Walsh stating they were out of ammunition and therefore unable to continue hunting. Ordered not to interfere with Indians hunting buffalo, Denny issued ammunition, tea, and tobacco in an effort to encourage them to remain on the plains. Even though it did little to advance the goal of "civilization," Canadian officials preferred to have the Cree hunting in Montana than congregating at Fort Walsh. Some of the Cree seem to have taken the ammunition Denny offered and promptly returned across the border. At about the same time Denny submitted his report, Agent Lincoln reported members of Piapot's and Little Pine's bands near the Fort Belknap agency.[29]

Apparently undeterred by the threat of expulsion, by November Cree from as far away as Edmonton had formed a large camp of about two hundred fifty lodges along the Milk River under the leadership of Little Pine and Lucky Man. According to Agent Denny, though, some of the Natives gathered near Fort Walsh seemed afraid to cross the border, frightened perhaps by rumours of Montana cattlemen hanging some Cree men for horse stealing. Other Cree bands likely avoided capture because, just as the Lakota had done in previous years, they remained camped just north of the border, crossing only in small parties in order to trade or hunt. In August a large group of Cree camped just north of the international boundary, where they were able to hunt buffalo and obtain alcohol and other goods from traders at Fort Assinniboine, either directly or through Métis traders in a large camp located immediately south of the border.[30]

When news of the army's patrols reached Ottawa, it provoked an indignant response from Canadian Deputy Superintendent General of Indian Affairs Lawrence Vankoughnet. "The conduct on the part of the American troops," he stated, "is at direct variance with the statement made in the Message of the President of the United States to the effect that the United States troops had been ordered to avoid for the present any collision with alien Indians." In fall 1881 Canadian officials apparently secured U.S. authorities' grudging acceptance that tribes could continue to cross the "imaginary boundary line in search of their means of subsistence."[31]

The issue of how to prevent cross-border stock raiding persisted. In 1882 Indian Commissioner Dewdney proposed a permit system that would allow groups such as the Blackfeet and Assiniboine, whose territories the border bisected, to move across it for hunting, visiting relatives, and other peaceful purposes. The Cree, who only travelled into Montana to hunt buffalo, would no longer have legitimate reason to move south, and Indian agents could therefore refuse to issue them permits.[32]

The capture of Sheriff Healy by a group of Métis and Saulteaux in March 1882 soon overshadowed discussions of the permit system and provoked another round of army manoeuvres. In February, Healy had received a special appointment granting him the power to seize the property of those he found trading illegally with Natives. He set out for the Métis settlements along the Milk River, intending to stop the Métis' illicit whisky trading and cross-border merchandise smuggling. After spending two weeks in the settlements looking for evidence under the guise of collecting taxes, Healy seized buffalo robes worth about $2,000 and arrested three men on charges of smuggling. The next night a group of about eighty Métis and Saulteaux surrounded Healy's cabin, freed the prisoners, retook the robes, and took Healy captive. On March 8 Captain O. B. Read arrived from the army's Poplar River camp and secured Healy's release. The Métis, however, quickly fled across the international boundary with the robes.[33]

Even before this potentially explosive situation, the U.S. government had resolved to force foreign Indians out of the country. Emphasizing this, Secretary of State Frederick Frelinghuysen informed the Canadian government that all Indian or Métis camps the army encountered would be broken up, their property destroyed, and their inhabitants forced across the border. After Healy's release, commanders ordered additional Fort Assinniboine soldiers to drive out all Canadian Indians and Métis. On March 14 troops compelled thirty-seven lodges of Cree under the leadership of Little Pine across the border. The next day troops set fire to 250 houses in a Métis and Indian settlement whose inhabitants had already fled north. For the remainder of the month, the army scoured the countryside in search of remaining camps. The Fort Benton *Benton Record* enthusiastically reported troops' attempts to chase down the Cree immediately following Sheriff Healy's release, but the triumph soured within a few weeks. By early May the newspaper reported that the Medicine Lodge country was again "overrun" with Métis, Saulteaux, and Cree. Throughout the summer, the army and the Cree played cat and mouse along the border.[34]

Those Cree who remained in the borderlands faced increasingly desperate circumstances. Some had returned to Fort Walsh months earlier after having had little luck hunting buffalo. Others, chased out by U.S. troops, began to arrive in wretched condition in April 1882. Determined to drive tribes away from the post, North West Mounted Police Commissioner Irvine refused to supply food and pressured the assembled chiefs to move with their bands north onto reserves. With game depleted in the vicinity of the Cypress Hills, little clothing or ammunition, few horses, and officials determined to issue as few rations as possible, many no doubt felt they had little choice but to leave. A number of the chiefs, including Piapot, moved onto reserves near Qu'Appelle in June while others went to Battleford.[35]

As Fort Walsh officials grew frustrated with Big Bear, Foremost Man, Lucky Man, and others who refused to move north, they began to take increasingly draconian measures. Irvine stated his intention to starve the remaining non-treaty Indians and those who refused to move north. Officials cut rations again in late June and informed nearby Indians of the agency's closure and cessation of payments there. The government shut agency farms and refused to survey any of the reserves previously promised to the various Cree and Assiniboine bands in the Cypress Hills.[36]

Despite this, approximately two thousand Indians assembled at Fort Walsh in September 1882, insisting that the Cypress Hills was their country. Piapot again joined them. He claimed that the promises made to him when he left in the spring had not been met and that his people were dying from starvation on their reserve.[37]

North West Mounted Police surgeon Augustus Jukes visited the Fort Walsh camp in October and described its miserable conditions. The scarcity of buffalo left the Indians without food, clothing, or shelter. Many crowded into lodges made only of lodge poles and spruce bows where, with barely more than rags as clothing, they huddled together for warmth. Jukes warned of disaster unless payments allowed them to secure provisions. Reports of starvation failed to move Indian Commissioner Dewdney. He chided North West Mounted Police Commissioner Irvine that he had been repeatedly instructed to inform the Cree and others that they would not be paid at Fort Walsh or receive reserves in the region since "the Southern Country is not the country of the Crees." He told Irvine that "the longer they continue to act against the wishes of the Govt the more wretched they will become."[38]

Those Cree who remained in the Cypress Hills had little choice but to search for game, and Big Bear, Lucky Man, and Little Pine departed for the plains, promising not to cross into the United States. No longer convinced that allowing the Cree to remain in Montana served Canadian interests, authorities at Fort Walsh began to work more closely with their counterparts at Fort Assinniboine. For instance, North West Mounted Police Commissioner Irvine, skeptical of Big Bear's promise to remain in Canada, maintained a close correspondence with Fort Assinniboine officials, keeping them abreast of the Crees' movements. He confided to Indian Commissioner Dewdney that he hoped the American troops would catch the Cree if they moved into the United States and "give them a sound thrashing."[39]

The Canadian government's tactics eventually achieved the desired effect. Although Dewdney relented and allowed the payment of treaty annuities at Fort Walsh in November 1882, Allan McDonald, the Indian agent in charge of the payments, expressed his desire to "punish" the Indians, and he gave them barely enough rations to survive. Non-treaty Indians received no assistance from the government. Faced with starvation, many followers of Big Bear broke with their chief and accepted treaty annuities. In December 1882, Big Bear, the last plains chief to sign a treaty, himself signed Treaty No. 6. Although a number of chiefs moved with their bands onto reserves, Big Bear remained in the Cypress Hills through the winter, subsisting on rations issued to prevent him and his followers from starving.[40]

Just how many Cree remained in the borderlands during winter 1882–83 remained unclear. In December, Secretary of State Frelinghuysen forwarded complaints from Captain Read, the commanding officer at the Poplar River post, that the Milk River country was "overrun with half-breeds, Crees, hostile Indians and armed Yanktonais," something which North West Mounted Police Inspector A. R. Macdonell, stationed just north at Wood Mountain, hotly denied. The conflicting estimates reflected, in part, the difficulties both governments faced as they attempted to enforce the international boundary. Army patrols scouted the Milk River country throughout the winter, occasionally encountering Cree and Métis parties, although at the same time, scouting parties also rode out but could find no trace of foreign Indians. The area's sheer size no doubt foiled the patrols, but confusion as to who ought to be ejected also likely played a part. As Macdonell pointed out, some of the Métis sighted were likely American mixed-bloods visiting relatives at Wood Mountain.[41]

The Cree who remained in the borderlands in winter 1882–83 found few buffalo, and conditions for Montana agency Indians looked equally grim. Fort Peck agent N. S. Porter and Fort Belknap agent W. L. Lincoln reported that white hunters, foreign Indians, and prairie fires prevented the agencies' Indians from killing their usual numbers of buffalo. They apparently secured most of their meat from the carcasses left by white hide hunters. Congressional reductions to the agencies' appropriations and crop failures exacerbated the food shortage. By summer 1883 the agents for the three agencies warned Commissioner of Indian Affairs Hiram Price of the threat of starvation. Indeed, between one-fourth and one-sixth of the Peigan in Montana died during winter 1882–83.[42]

Perhaps because they expected that they would soon leave the borderlands, the Cree carried out a series of raids against Montana Peigan, Gros Ventre, and Assiniboine in spring 1883. One of the most daring occurred in March under the leadership of Cut Foot. After breaking into two parties, one group of Cree captured approximately fifty horses from Joe Kipp's ranch along the Marias River while the other stole twenty-one horses from an outfit near Willow Round. The Cree quickly made for the border, but a party of Peigan and white men started in pursuit. Three Cree men died in the ensuing fight. The surviving raiders escaped across the border with the stolen horses and arrived at Fort Walsh on March 21. The following week the Blackfeet and Fort Belknap agents reported Cree raiders stole sixty-seven head of horses from the Gros Ventre and 111 ponies from the Blackfeet agency during March.[43]

Faced with persistent cross-border raids, Secretary of State Frelinghuysen informed Canadian officials that the proposed permit system would do nothing to address the problem of Indians who raided in Montana and fled across the border. He enclosed instead a copy of an agreement reached between the

United States and Mexico allowing for the reciprocal right to pursue Indians across the border and suggested a similar Canadian-American arrangement. Bristling at the suggestion of U.S. troops crossing freely into Canada, Indian Commissioner Dewdney responded that, while the Canadian government had no objection to the seizure and destruction of raiding parties' property, cross-border raids were diminishing and would cease completely by the coming winter as the Canadian government compelled all Cree to move north.[44]

In the meantime, Canadian officials sought new ways to end these raids. North West Mounted Police Superintendent A. Shurtliff had warned Cut Foot that if he crossed the border with hostile intent, he would be arrested and the stolen stock taken away. When two Montana cattle outfit employees followed a war party back to Fort Walsh, Shurtliff made good on his promise. However, he could recover only seven stolen horses. The Cree cached the remainder in the hills near the fort and refused to give them up, saying they were needed to offset the killing of their three companions. On May 8, 1883, Lt. Col. James Macleod and North West Mounted Police Commissioner Irvine convicted eleven of the men of transporting stolen property across the border and sentenced them to two years of hard labour at Stony Mountain Penitentiary in Manitoba. As part of the Canadian government's strategy to force the Cree away from the Cypress Hills, officials promised Cree chiefs that if they moved north and continued to behave themselves the men would be released.[45]

The second part of the strategy to induce the Cree to stay in Canada included the abandonment of Fort Walsh in May 1883. After years of deliberation, the Canadian government finally moved its North West Mounted Police post to Maple Creek, northeast of the Cypress Hills. With game depleted and government rations unavailable, remaining near the border held fewer opportunities for Cree bands. Most had little choice but to move north. In June and July, North West Mounted Police escorts accompanied the bands led by Big Bear, Little Pine, and Lucky Man north to Battleford where they were expected to select reserves. When a small number of Cree used buckboards given to them by the Department of Indian Affairs to return to Maple Creek that summer, the North West Mounted Police forced most of them to move to their reserves by threatening arrest under the terms of Canada's Vagrant Act. Through the concerted actions of both federal governments, the majority of the Cree vacated the borderlands by 1884. Not all left, however. Foremost Man and his followers remained in the borderlands without government assistance for years. The government finally established a reserve for the band near Maple Creek, Saskatchewan, in 1913.[46]

In 1885 the Northwest Rebellion, a conflict that arose out of disagreement between the region's Métis and the Canadian government over Métis land rights, subsumed a number of local conflicts involving various Indian bands and embroiled some Cree in the events that would once again force them to look to the borderlands. In the small settlement of Frog Lake (northeast of Edmonton) several Cree men from Big Bear's band killed nine people on April 2, 1885, and took the remainder of the white settlers captive. In response to the incident, which occurred just weeks after Louis Riel's declaration of a provisional government, the Canadian government mobilized its forces to quell the uprising. In the aftermath of encounters with Canadian troops, most of the Cree associated with Big Bear's camp surrendered or sought refuge with other bands. However, Lucky Man, Little Poplar, and Little Bear (Imasees) and their families sought asylum in the United States.

By October 1885 several Cree families had arrived at Fort Belknap, and Agent Lincoln again pressed officials in Washington to expel the Cree from the territory. American Secretary of State T. F. Bayard responded that unless Canadian authorities demanded the return of the Cree refugees under the extradition treaty, U.S. authorities could not force them across the border. Canadian authorities worried that asking U.S. authorities to surrender the Cree, who occupied a position similar to the refugee Lakota who had fled to Canada in 1876–77, would create a dangerous precedent. No request was forthcoming. Over the next several years, the Cree lived in small camps scattered across Montana where they struggled to eke out an existence. Although other Canadian Cree joined these refugees after 1885, their numbers never again reached the size of those of 1879–81.[47]

The need to distinguish and classify a diverse mix of people and to make them fit within the broader policy goals underlay the attempts by Washington and Ottawa to restrict the cross-border movement of the Plains Cree in the 1880s. While the combination of converging national interests and the collapse of the buffalo economy made the restriction of the cross-border movement of the Cree possible, the Crees' persistence across Montana and the continued arrival of small groups from Canada suggests that crossing the border remained an option for the Cree through the end of the nineteenth century. Their continued presence in the borderlands demonstrates that the use of the border to mark nationality remained incomplete.

NOTES

1 Record of Events, Fort Assinniboine (hereafter Record of Events, Fort Assinniboine), November 1881, roll 42, microfilm M617; Returns from U.S. Military Posts, Fort Assinniboine, 1879–91, Record Group 94 (hereafter RG 94); Records of the Adjutant General's Office, National Archives and Records Administration, Washington D.C. (hereafter NARA); Cecil E. Denny to Indian Commissioner, November 16, 1881, file 29506-1, vol. 3744, Record Group 10 (hereafter RG 10); Department of Indian Affairs fonds, National Archives of Canada, Ottawa, Ontario (hereafter NAC); Cecil E. Denny to Edgar Dewdney, November 20, 1881, ibid.; Cecil E. Denny to Assistant Indian Commissioner, December 6, 1881, ibid. The North-West Territories encompassed present-day Alberta and Saskatchewan.

2 Although Canada had achieved its political independence from Great Britain in 1867, Britain retained control over foreign policy until 1931.

3 William A. Fraser, "Plains Cree, Assiniboine and Saulteaux (Plains) Bands, 1874–84," 1963, TS, pp. 4–6, Collection M4379, Glenbow Archives, Calgary, Alberta (hereafter Glenbow).

4 Patricia C. Albers, "Changing Patterns of Ethnicity in the Northeastern Plains, 1780–1870," in *History, Power, and Identity: Ethnogenesis in the Americas, 1492–1992*, ed. Jonathan D. Hill (Iowa City, IA: University of Iowa Press, 1996), 109–11; Regna Darnell, "Plains Cree," in *Handbook of North American Indians*, ed. Raymond J. DeMallie, vol. 13 (Washington, D.C., 2001), 642.

5 Fraser, "Plains Cree, Assiniboine," 7–8, 10–11; Edwin Denig, *Five Indian Tribes of the Upper Missouri: Northern Plains Sioux, Arickaras, Assiniboines, Crees, Crows* (Norman: University of Oklahoma Press, 1961), 110–11; Hugh A. Dempsey, "Maskepetoon," in *Dictionary of Canadian Biography*, vol. 9 (Toronto: University of Toronto Press, 1976), 537.

6 Hugh A. Dempsey, *Big Bear: The End of Freedom* (Vancouver, 1984), 89–95; Sarah Carter, *Lost Harvests: Prairie Indian Reserve Farmers and Government Policy* (Montreal: McGill-Queen's Press, 1990), 58–61, 71.

7 Michael P. Malone, Richard B. Roeder, and William L. Lang, *Montana: A History of Two Centuries*, rev. ed. (Seattle: University of Washington Press, 1991), 120–21, 13941. In 1873 President Ulysses S. Grant by executive order reserved the land north of the Missouri and Sun rivers between Dakota territory and the Continental Divide as Indian territory.

8 Robert Utley, *The Lance and the Shield: The Life and Times of Sitting Bull* (New York, 1993), 181–82; David G. McCrady, "Living with Strangers: The Nineteenth-Century Sioux and the Canadian-American Borderlands" (Ph.D. diss., University of Manitoba, 1998), 125–28, 144–45. The Lakota also required the goodwill of neighbouring tribes whose territories they inhabited in order to continue to live and hunt in the region.

9   Nicholas P. Hardeman, "Brick Stronghold of the Border: Fort Assinniboine, 1879–1911," *Montana The Magazine of Western History* 29 (spring 1979): 56; Merrill G. Burlingame, *The Montana Frontier* (Bozeman, MT: 1980), 243–44; Joseph Manzione, *"I am Looking to the North for My Life": Sitting Bull, 1876–1881* (Salt Lake City: University of Utah Press, 1991), 15.

10   U.S. House, Report of the Secretary of War, 46th Cong., 2d sess., 1879–1880, H. Doc. 1, pt. 2:76; Elliot T. Galt to Edgar Dewdney, March 22, 1880, file 20,140, vol. 3712, RG 10, NAC. The Fort Benton (MT) *Benton Record* echoed these sentiments on June 20, 1879.

11   Sir John A. Macdonald to Lord Lorne, May 15, 1880, pp. 31605–8, vol. 81, Manuscript Group 26A, Sir John A. Macdonald Papers, NAC (hereafter Macdonald Papers); James F. Macleod to J. S. Dennis, August 9, 1879, pt. 1, file 8589, vol. 3652, RG 10, NAC; Clerk, Privy Council to Minister of Interior, September 22, 1879, ibid.; Manzione, *"I am Looking to the North for My Life,"* 135–37.

12   Hugh A. Dempsey, *Crowfoot: Chief of the Blackfeet* (Edmonton, AB: 1976), 115; D. L. MacPherson to Edgar Dewdney, May 22, 1881, pp. 1176–77, vol. 5, Collection M320, Edgar Dewdney fonds (hereafter Dewdney fonds), Glenbow; D. L. MacPherson to Edgar Dewdney, July 15, 1881, pp. 1172–75, ibid.

13   U.S. House, Report of the Secretary of War, 1879–1880, pt. 2:61–63; Joseph Manzione, *"I am Looking to the North for My Life,"* 135; Edward Thornton to Marquis of Salisbury, October 13, 1879, pt. 1, file 8589, vol. 3652, RG 10, NAC; Canada, House of Commons, Sessional Papers, 1881, no. 14, p. 81; James F. Macleod to Deputy Minister of the Interior, November 24, 1879, pt. 1, file 8589, vol. 3652, RG 10, NAC.

14   J. W. Schultz, *My Life as an Indian: The Story of a Red Woman and a White Man in the Lodges of the Blackfeet* (New York: Doubleday, Page & Company, 1907), 378. In 1869–70 Riel led the Métis resistance against the Canadian government's acquisition of the Hudson's Bay Company's territory.

15   Acheson G. Irvine to Officer Commanding, Fort Assinniboine, June 14, 1882, pp. 580–83, vol. 2235, Record Group 18, Royal Canadian Mounted Police fonds, NAC (hereafter RG 18); Edwin Allen to Edgar Dewdney, October 15, 1880, file 24827, vol. 3726, RG 10, NAC.

16   Granville Stuart, *Forty Years on the Frontier, as seen in the Journals and Reminiscences of Granville Stuart*, ed. Paul C. Phillips, 2 vols. (Cleveland, OH: Arthur H. Clark Company, 1925), 2:153–54. Canadian authorities dismissed Stuart's claims as exaggerated. Lord Lorne to [unknown], n.d., file 28748-1, vol. 3740, RG 10, NAC; Edgar Dewdney to Sir John [A. Macdonald], October 26, 1881, pp. 89596–604, vol. 210, Macdonald Papers, NAC; Dempsey, *Big Bear*, 93, 97–99; Dempsey, *Crowfoot*, 124–25.

17   Cecil E. Denny to Assistant Indian Commissioner, December 6, 1881, file 29506-2, vol. 3744, RG 10, NAC; James F. Macleod to J. S. Dennis, December 1, 1879, pt. 1, file 8589, vol. 3652, ibid.; Edgar Dewdney to Sir John A. Macdonald,

December 24, 1879, pp. 89310–12, vol. 210, Macdonald Papers, NAC; Thomas Flanagan, *Louis "David" Riel: Prophet of the New World* (Toronto: University of Toronto Press, 1979), 105–6.

18 John C. Ewers, "Ethnological Report on the Chippewa Cree Tribe of the Rocky Boy Reservation and the Little Shell Band of Indians," in *Chippewa Indians*, vol. 6 (New York: Garland Publishing, 1974), 77. See also Annual Report of the Commissioner of Indian Affairs (Washington, D.C., 1879), 98; Fort Benton (MT), *Benton Weekly Record*, July 16, 1880.

19 W. L. Lincoln to E. A. Hayt, June 16, 1879, pt. 1, file 8589, vol. 3652, RG 10, NAC; U.S. House, *Report of the Secretary of War*, 1879–1880, pt. 2:70.

20 John L. Tobias, "Canada's Subjugation of the Plains Cree, 1879–1885," *Canadian Historical Review*, 64, no. 4 (1983), 527–28; Carter, *Lost Harvests*, 111–12; A. B. McCullough, *Papers Relating to the North-West Mounted Police and Fort Walsh* (Ottawa, 1977), 68.

21 Dempsey, *Big Bear*, 100; Edwin Allen to Edgar Dewdney, May 1881, file 29506-1, vol. 3744, RG 10, NAC; Elliot T. Galt to Edwin Allen, May 20, 1881, ibid.; Elliot T. Galt to D. L. MacPherson, July 14, 1881, pp. 89498–503, vol. 210, Macdonald Papers, NAC.

22 Canada, House of Commons, *Sessional Papers*, 1881, no. 14, pp. 105–7.

23 Elliot T. Galt to Wadsworth, July 13, 1881, file 29506-1, vol. 3744, RG 10, NAC; Elliot T. Galt to Lawrence Vankoughnet, July 13, 1881, ibid.; Thomas P. Wadsworth to Elliot T. Galt, July 28, 1881, pp. 89552–53, vol. 210, Macdonald Papers, NAC; Thomas P. Wadsworth to Elliot T. Galt, July 31, 1881, pp. 89557–58, ibid.; Thomas P. Wadsworth to Elliot T. Galt, August 8, 1881, file 29506-1, vol. 3744, RG 10, NAC.

24 R. N. Wilson diary, August 11, 20, 1881, Manuscript Group 29 E47, NAC; Elliot T. Galt to Superintendent General of Indian Affairs August 23, 1881, file 29506-1, vol. 3744, RG 10, NAC; *Battleford (Sask.) Saskatchewan Herald*, May 23, 1881; Thomas P. Wadsworth to Elliot T. Galt, July 25, 1881, pp. 89546–50, vol. 210, Macdonald Papers, NAC.

25 Wadsworth to Galt, July 25, 1881; Acheson G. Irvine to Frederick White, August 14, 1881, pp. 260–67, vol. 2186, RG 18, NAC; Thomas P. Wadsworth to Lawrence Vankoughnet, August 29, 1881, file 29506-1, vol. 3744, RG 10, NAC; Canada, House of Commons, *Sessional Papers*, 1881, no. 3, p 33. Other rationale given for closing Fort Walsh included the unsuitability of the surrounding countryside for agriculture, the poor condition of the fort, the lack of white settlement in the region, and its dependence on Fort Benton merchants for its supplies. Critics argued that too much government money was being funneled into the hands of American merchants.

26 Fort Benton (MT), *Benton Weekly Record*, August 18, September 15, 29, November 17, 1881; Sharp, *Whoop-Up Country*, 234; Burlingame, *Montana Frontier*, 267–68. Dewdney disputed allegations that Canadian Indians were responsible for the majority of depredations in northern Montana. See Edgar

Dewdney to Sir John [A. Macdonald], October 26, 1881, pp. 89596–604, vol. 210, Macdonald Papers, NAC.

27   U.S. House, *Report of the Secretary of War*, 47th Cong., 1st sess., 1881, H. Doc. 1, pt. 2:110; Thomas Ruger to Officer Commanding, Fort Assinaboine, September 14, 1881, folder 3, box 1, Manuscript Collection 46, Fort Assinniboine Records (hereafter Fort Assinniboine Records), Montana Historical Society Archives, Helena (hereafter MHS). See also Record of Events, Fort Assinniboine, October 1881.

28   Record of Events, Fort Assinniboine, October 1881; Gustavus Doane to [his wife], October 13, 22, 1881, Small Collection 28, Gustavus Doane Papers, MHS (hereafter Doane Papers).

29   Edgar Dewdney to Cecil E. Denny, October [2], 1881, file 33527 vol. 3768, RG 10, NAC; Cecil E. Denny to Edgar Dewdney, November 1, 1881, file 29506-1, vol. 3744, ibid.; Cecil E. Denny to [Edgar Dewdney], November 9, 1881, ibid.; W. L. Lincoln to R. L. Morris, November 2, 1881, folder 3, box 1, Fort Assinniboine Records, MHS.

30   Denny to Dewdney, November 1, 1881; Cecil E. Denny to [Edgar Dewdney], November 9, 1881, file 29506-1, vol. 3744, RG 10, NAC; John H. McIllree to Commanding Officer, Fort Assinaboine, September 14, 1881, pp. 344–45, vol. 2235, RG 18, NAC; Cecil E. Denny to Indian Commissioner, November 16, 1881.

31   Lawrence Vankoughnet to Sir John A. Macdonald, December 13, 1881, file 29506-1, vol. 3744, RG 10, NAC; Privy Council to Minister of the Interior, June 3, 1881, pt. 1, file 8589, vol. 3652, ibid.; Edward Thornton to Earl Granville, May 16, 1881, file 28748-1, vol. 3740, ibid.; Alexander Campbell to [Privy Council Office], September 13, 1881, ibid.

32   Lieutenant Colonel de Winton to Privy Council, March 3, 1882, file 28748-1, vol. 3740, RG 10, NAC; Edgar Dewdney to Superintendent General of Indian Affairs, March 27, 1882, ibid.

33   Fort Benton (MT), *Benton Weekly Record*, March 16, 23, 30, 1882.

34   [L. S. Sackville West] to Marquis of Lorne, February 28, 1882, file 28748-1, vol. 3740, RG 10, NAC; Record of Events, Fort Assinniboine March 1882; U.S. House, *Report of the Secretary of War*, 47th Cong., 2d sess., 1882, H. Doc. 1, pt. 2: 85–87, 94–95; Fort Benton (MT) *Benton Weekly Record*, March 30, May 4, 1882; Gustavus Doane to [his wife], July 10, 13, 1882, Doane Papers, MHS. See also U.S. House, *Report of the Secretary of War*, 1882, pt. 2, pp. 83–92, for a summary of these manoeuvres for 1882.

35   Acheson G. Irvine to Frederick White, June 28, 1882, pp. 711–22, vol. 2186, RG 18, NAC; McCullough, *Papers relating to the North-West Mounted Police*, 72–73.

36   Tobias, "Canada's Subjugation of the Plains Cree," 530–31; Battleford Fort (Sask.) *Saskatchewan Herald*, May 27, June 24, 1882.

37 Acheson G. Irvine to Edgar Dewdney, September 23, 1882, file 29506-2, vol. 3744, RG 10, NAC; Canada, House of Commons, *Sessional Papers*, 1883, no. 23, pp. 4–5; Carter, *Lost Harvests*, 122–23.

38 Augustus Jukes to Frederick White, October 17, 1882, file 29506-2, vol. 3744, RG 10, NAC; Edgar Dewdney to Acheson G. Irvine, October 27, 1882, ibid.

39 Canada, House of Commons, *Sessional Papers*, 1883, no. 23, p. 4; John H. McIllree to Indian Commissioner, June 21 1882, file 2589, vol. 3604, RG 10, NAC; Acheson G. Irvine to Edgar Dewdney, June 24, 1882, pp. 1193–1200, vol. 5, Dewdney fonds, Glenbow; Irvine to Officer Commanding, Fort Assinniboine, June 21, 1882, pp. 620–22, vol. 2235, RG 18, NAC; Acheson G. Irvine to Frederick White, June 28, 1882, 711–22, vol. 2186, ibid.

40 Allan MacDonald to [unknown], November 11, 1882, file 29506-3, vol. 3744, RG 10, NAC; Canada, House of Commons, *Sessional Papers*, 1883, no. 5, p. xi.

41 Frederick J. Frelinghuysen to L. S. Sackville West, December 20, 1882, file 8, vol. 1004, RG 18, NAC; A. R. Macdonell to Commissioner, North West Mounted Police, January 20, 1883, file 24A, ibid.; A. R. Macdonnell to Acheson G. Irvine, November 30, 1883, file 28748-1, vol. 3740, RG 10, NAC; Thomas H. Ruger to Adjutant General, April 25, 1883, file 28748-2, ibid.

42 *Annual Report of the Commissioner of Indian Affairs* (Washington, DC, 1882), 105, 110; *Annual Report of the Commissioner of Indian Affairs*, 1879, lix; John C. Ewers, *The Blackfeet: Raiders on the North-Western Plains* (Norman, 1958), 294.

43 William Rowe to Thomas H. Ruger, March 23, 1883, file 28748-1, vol. 3740, RG 10, NAC; Guido Ilges to Assistant Adjutant General, April 8, 1883, file 28748-2, ibid.; Fort Benton (MT) *Benton Weekly Record*, March 24, 1883; W. L. Lincoln to Guido Ilges, April 3, 1883, file 28748-2, vol. 3740, RG 10, NAC; John Young to Thomas Ruger, April 4, 1883, ibid.

44 Frederick J. Frelinghuysen to L. S. Sackville West, April 17, 1883, pt. 4A, file 2001, vol. 319, series G21, Record Group 7, Office of the Governor General of Canada fonds, NAC; Edgar Dewdney to [Privy Council Office], April 1883, file 28748-1, vol. 3740, RG 10, NAC.

45 Ilges to Assistant Adjutant General, April 8, 1883; Acheson G. Irvine to Edgar Dewdney, December 24, 1883, file 28748-2, vol. 3740, RG 10, NAC; Dempsey, *Big Bear*, 112; Hayter Reed to Indian Commissioner, December 28, 1883, file 10644, vol. 3668, RG 10, NAC. Prior to 1880, only one Indian man was convicted and sentenced for horse stealing in Canada. The severity of sentencing Indians for this crime increased dramatically after 1880. See Brian Hubner, "Horse Stealing and the Borderline: The NWMP and the Control of Indian Movement, 1874–1900," in *The Mounted Police and Prairie Society, 1873–1919*, ed. William Baker (Regina, SK: Canadian Plains Research Centre, 1998), 63–64.

46 Dempsey, *Big Bear*, 112; Canada, House of Commons, Sessional Papers, 1884, no. 4, pp. 98–99; ibid., no. 125, 15–16; David Lee, "Foremost Man and his Band," *Saskatchewan History*, 36 (Autumn 1983), 100.

47   Blair Stonechild and Bill Waiser, *Loyal Till Death: Indians and the North-West Rebellion* (Calgary, AB: Fifth House Publishers, 1997), 190–91, 194; U.S. House, *Cree Indians, Montana*, 49th Cong., 1st sess., 1886, H. Doc. 231, 2–3; Superintendent General of Indian Affairs (SGIA) to Privy Council, January 26, 1887, file 36563, vol. 3774, RG 10, NAC.

Chapter 6

Making the Forty-Ninth Parallel: How Canada and the United States Used Space, Race, and Gender to Turn Blackfoot Country into the Alberta-Montana Borderlands

Sheila McManus, University of Lethbridge

It took less than half a century to turn Blackfoot country at the northwestern corner of the Great Plains into the Alberta-Montana borderlands. Although the United States and England had agreed in 1818 that the forty-ninth parallel would be the border across the west, in 1850 the land east of the Rockies between about present-day Edmonton, Alberta and Helena, Montana was still a poorly-mapped "wilderness," firmly in the hands of the three tribes of the Blackfoot Confederacy: the Peigan or Piikuni, the Blood or Kainah, and the Blackfoot proper or Siksika. By 1900 the region had been surveyed, subdivided, and was quickly being handed over to white male farmers, ranchers, and railroad companies, while the Blackfoot had been reduced to starvation and poverty on small, disconnected reserves. Along the way, Canada and the United States had faced the same three problems: gaining control of the land, gaining control of the original owners of the land, and then finding the "right" kind of people to fill up those big spaces. They also shared a common colonial tool kit, having at their disposal everything from maps, surveys, and legislation to armed force and the distribution of rations.

Each government responded to these problems with a range of policies based on assumptions about space, race, and gender. In the 1850s Ottawa and Washington assumed that the Blackfoot were taking up too much space, and so they would have to be forced to take up less space so that a greater number of white men could put the land to "better" use. By the 1880s, both governments became concerned that certain white men were now taking up too much space, and they too had to be forced to take up less. The goal in both cases was to maximize the number of 160-acre portions that could be turned over to white male farmers. Throughout the late nineteenth century, white officials also assumed that Aboriginal people were "uncivilized," inferior, and less entitled to their land than white people because white people would turn the "unproductive wilderness" into 160-acre family farms. There was the further assumption that the traditional Blackfoot masculinity based on hunting and horse raids had to give way to the white European masculinity of farming; not only was the latter considered superior, but it also took up less space and was more sedentary. These assumptions are evident and intertwined in Canadian and American attitudes towards Blackfoot country in the late nineteenth century, and were instrumental in the region's transformation.

This article focuses on the key years between the late 1860s and mid-1880s to explore how this transition was accomplished, where the governments "succeeded" and where they failed. It examines how each national government perceived and tried to consolidate its hold over "its" West and "its" side of the border through this grid of racialized and gendered policies. It argues that the transition was uneven, always contested, and never quite as successful as federal officials wanted and believed it to be. The amount that they did manage to accomplish, however, was remarkable, and in less than thirty years the foundation was laid for the settler society that was to follow.[1]

The 1860s, 1870s, and 1880s were eventful years in Blackfoot country. Montana became a Territory in 1864, and in 1870 the Canadian government finally took over the North-West Territories from the Hudson's Bay Company, acquiring almost overnight an area five times larger than the area of the original Dominion. Also in 1870 the American army slaughtered 173 Piikuni men, women, and children on the Marias River just south of the forty-ninth parallel. The army had been authorized to attack a Piikuni band that was rumoured to contain "troublemakers," but attacked a peaceful band instead. In 1873 the Department of the Interior and the North West Mounted Police were created by the Government of Canada to manage the land and people at the western edge of the Prairies. After three earlier treaties had been ignored by the United States, the Blackfoot of Montana were finally given an official reservation in 1874, although it would be whittled down for the next twenty years. The Blackfoot in Alberta signed Treaty No. 7 in 1877. The Northern Pacific made it to Helena in 1883 and Canadian Pacific Railway arrived in Calgary in 1884.

Each of these "events" played a role in helping the Canadian and American governments consolidate their hold over the region. When North American bureaucrats wrote about the West in the mid-nineteenth century, their preferred adjectives were words like "immense" and "limitless" – positive characteristics in the minds of colonial governments. But first they had to control it somehow, find ways to manage and administer such vastness. They employed surveys to impose a grid of borders and boundaries, and censuses to figure out who was already living there. They sought an interlocking grid of knowledge and control, the thoroughness of which would allow each state, as Benedict Anderson has suggested, "to always be able to say of anything that it was this, not that; it belonged here, not there."[2]

Until the completion of the railroads on either side of the forty-ninth parallel gave eastern bureaucrats a semblance of direct control over western lands, they had to be content with other ways of controlling and managing what they saw when they looked west. The preferred technique was information-gathering: exploring and mapping and surveying western lands as a substitute for and precursor of actual hands-on control. And what the surveys and maps and reports told bureaucrats allowed them to continually reframe their visions of Blackfoot country, as the "desert wastelands" of the 1850s gave way to the "fertile valleys" of the 1870s and the "best stock ranges in the world" in the 1880s. This shift was accompanied and created by ever-more-localized information and supervision.

There is a decided ambivalence in the reports of the Canadian and American bureaucrats who wrote about the land east of the Rockies in the

1870s. For the Americans the West, somehow just by existing, was proof of the greatness of the Republic. Joseph Wilson, commissioner of the General Lands Office, declared in 1870 that "the end of the present century will probably witness the development of a world-wide social system, a reciprocity of trade, and a systematic development of industry in all the nations of the earth. This glorious consummation will be largely due to the acquisition and disposal of our public domain by the General Government. No one influence has so broadened the area of free society."[3]

For the Canadians, their newly acquired domain meant that someday they would also be a great nation. In his report for 1883 Canada's Deputy Minister of the Interior A. M. Burgess was pleased to note that the amount of land surveyed and subdivided in the West that year was "equal to 168,750 farms of 160 acres each." He calculated that this translated into an area "capable of accommodating a purely agricultural population of 506,250, allowing an average of only three souls per farm – a result, I venture to submit, never before attained within a similar period of time in the history of any country, and one which is well calculated to exemplify the determination of the Government and the readiness of the people of Canada to spare neither energy nor money in order to open up the fertile lands of the North-West and make them available for settlement." In practical terms the 1883 surveys had also proved "beyond dispute that large tracts of land, represented upon the educational maps with which the present generation is familiar as useless desert, are found to be of good quality and well fitted for the varied branches of agriculture." He concluded that there did not seem to be any part "of the surveyed portions of the North-West upon which nature has not bestowed her favours lavishly."[4]

Both governments were sure the region would soon be settled by "millions" of whites. Yet, at times, that much space seemed like too much of a good thing: it had to be mapped, portioned-out, and controlled, and the indigenous population had an annoying habit of not standing still to be counted.

The difficulties seemed more overwhelming for American officials because white settlers headed west much more quickly than the surveyors. In 1867 Joseph Wilson, Commissioner of the General Land Office, noted that Montana Territory was "remote from the seat of the surveyor general's office" and because of "the unsettled condition of the plains, growing out of Indian incursions, it has been deemed proper to defer surveys in that Territory until the ensuing season."[5] When the surveys did begin in Montana, they moved quickly: by 1870 about 1.5 million of the Territory's ninety-two million acres had been surveyed. Wilson added that the territory was larger than the states of New York, Pennsylvania, and Ohio combined, and that the Rocky Mountains were its "most striking feature."[6]

Montana's topography and the behaviour of some of its inhabitants gave the surveyors several problems. In 1871 Willis Drummond, Wilson's successor as Commissioner of the General Land Office, wrote that "owing to the abrupt and mountainous character of a great portion of that Territory" the surveys were "to a considerable extent, disconnected, and have been restricted mainly to those detached bodies of lands available for actual settlement...." He assured his readers, however, that "great care" had been taken "to make the projection as regular as practicable."[7] The following year Montana's Surveyor-General John Blaine remarked that "On account of the mountains the surveys are very irregular; but they are all properly connected by standard and meridian lines, and projected according to the regular system of public land surveys."[8]

Making "abrupt" and "irregular" terrain conform was easier than getting some of the Territory's inhabitants to respect the resulting demarcations, however. In 1874 Blaine's successor, Andrew Smith, complained that a better way of marking the corners of the surveys was needed. "In a stock-country like our own," he wrote, "where cattle are numerous in every valley, and ranging all over the table-lands and hills adjacent," the system of supporting posts in mounds of earth was proving to be quite inadequate. He stated that the posts "stand but a few hours, in some instances but a few moments," before the cattle paw the mound away and rub down the post. In time, the posts are "either picked up and burned, used as a picket-pin, or removed far from its original position." And without fixed markers to "perpetuate" the corners of a survey, the integrity of the survey itself is at risk.[9]

In 1883 Canada's Surveyor-General Lindsay Russell echoed these complaints about the impermanence of the wooden markers, implying that everything from the elements to cattle to First Nations peoples were conspiring against their survival. Prairie fires burned the wooden posts in their mounds of earth; herds of cattle demolished the mounds; and then the spring run-off washed "the posts away and little or no trace of survey remains. They are even subject to being effaced through the ignorance or perversity of the natives of the prairie region, who, if hearsay is to be credited, have when travelling across a stretch of prairie, where other wood for fire could not easily be obtained, been seen provided with a goodly cart load of fuel consisting of township survey posts, gathered on their way." Iron posts had always been used to mark the corners of blocks of townships, but that the "additional expense … of placing iron posts at every township corner" was now being incurred to try and resolve the problem.[10]

Similar problems do not seem to have arisen with the cairns and posts used to mark the forty-ninth parallel, although it is possible that once the survey was complete neither side ever checked how the border's only physical evidence was holding up. Britain and the United States first agreed that the forty-ninth parallel would be the line dividing their respective western territories in 1818 – a quiet, bloodless division of an enormous amount of territory, apparently so unremarkable that it isn't even consistently mentioned in the average Canadian or American history textbook. More than half a century would pass before the two governments got around to actually surveying the border.

The North American Boundary Commission Survey was called the "International Boundary Commission" by the Canadian government and the "Northern Boundary Commission" by the Americans, and operated from 1872 to 1874. The forty-ninth parallel was surveyed and marked with cairns, and the commissions generated a great deal of information about the land in the immediate vicinity of the border. In 1875 David Laird, Canada's Minister of the Interior, was pleased to announce that the work of the Boundary Commission was complete. He concluded that "the authoritative determination of this missing link in our international boundary line cannot but be a source of satisfaction to the Imperial and Dominion Governments."[11] Once the survey was complete the Imperial and Dominion and even American governments may well have been satisfied that the missing link had been found and agreed-upon, finally confirming the separateness of their two countries. The governments felt they could now look west and know, at least, when they were looking at their own territory. However, drawing the line which was to separate one country from another was clearly a minor issue when compared with the bigger problems of incorporating "their" western lands into the national economy.

Both governments formulated a range of legislation designed to ensure western land looked and produced the way they wanted it to. The best-known policies are the United States' 1862 Homestead Act and Canada's 1872 Dominion Lands Act, both of which codified deeply held assumptions about space, race, and gender. Both were designed to parcel out western lands in 160-acre pieces, ideally to a white man who would turn it into a "family farm." By institutionalizing the ideal of a 160-acre farm with a white male at its head, it is clear that both governments expected and wanted the future to duplicate the past.[12] In Ontario or Ohio ample rainfall and timber meant that 160 acres was a good size for a "family farm." But in the northern Great Plains west of the hundredth meridian, 160 acres was too small to be a profitable ranch and too large to be a profitable non-irrigated farm.[13]

Both Acts were also clearly based on assumptions about the kind of person each government wanted to homestead the West. They assumed that it would be men who would head west and stake their claims, because the very ideal of "the family farm" privileged male agency and land-ownership. For example, Commissioner of the General Land Office Joseph Wilson, stated in his 1867 annual report that the "purpose" of the Homestead Act "is to hold out incentives for immigrants to identify themselves with the broad fields of the west, and secure their labour for such a period in the strength of manhood or maturity of life as will insure stability in settlements, development of arable resources, and steady increase of agricultural wealth."[14] His choice of language was hardly new – it was merely the 1860s version of United States President Thomas Jefferson's yeoman farmer transplanted onto the new vistas west of the Mississippi.

The one striking anomaly in each government's attitudes towards white women was that the American Act allowed unmarried women to take up homesteads on the same footing as men, while unmarried women were only able to do so for the first four years after the passage of Canada's 1872 legislation. The original Act did not restrict homesteading provisions to single men, but in his report for 1875, Canada's Surveyor-General J. S. Dennis indicated that he wanted "To render females, not being heads of families, ineligible to enter for homesteads" under the Dominion Lands Act.[15] The Act was amended in 1876 to specify "Any person, male or female, who is the sole head of a family, or any male, who has attained the age of eighteen years, shall be entitled to be entered for one quarter-section, or a less quantity, of unappropriated Dominion lands, for the purpose of securing a homestead right in respect thereof."[16] This revision entrenched the assumption that men and women were to have different relationships to Canada's western land, although even the American's more liberal legislation doesn't seem to have had a significant impact on the masculinity of the American West or the connection between masculinity and land-ownership.

Neither Ottawa nor Washington ever abandoned their overarching vision of the West as a region which should be filled with 160-acre family farms, but each government was forced to make some concessions when it came to the land which straddled the border east of the Rockies. The fact that the region was too dry for traditional forms of agriculture, however, was quickly turned into an advantage, and the land's potential for stock raising quickly became its chief selling point in the reports of Canadians and Americans alike. As an economic activity, land-use system and social system ranching is not compatible with 160-acre family farms because it involves very different uses of space and different combinations of race and gender. It can thrive on land with relatively little rain and tree cover, however, and thus even arid, treeless plains could be put to some use by white men and add to the wealth of the nation.

The United States clung more tightly to its agricultural, yeoman farmer ideal by passing the Desert Lands Act in 1877 which made it easier for individuals to get larger blocks of land west of the hundredth meridian if they promised to irrigate a portion of their holdings. Commissioner of the General Land Office S. S. Burdett noted in his 1875 report that between the hundredth meridian and the mountains, and "from the Mexican line on the south to the international boundary on the north, a totally different set of conditions, geographical, physical, and climatic, are found to exist. Within this vast area agriculture, as pursued in the valley of the Mississippi and to the eastward, has no existence. Irrigation is indispensable to production."[17] The alternative was to use the land for livestock, and massive ranches were common across the northern Great Plains, but the American government did not create policies to formally accommodate this use of western land the way Canada did.

Canada's concession to the dry, treeless environment in southern Alberta in the 1870s and 1880s was to bring in a system whereby ranchers could lease huge tracts of land in southern Alberta from the federal government for only pennies an acre. This system drew another line through western lands – the southwest corner of Canada's western interior was increasingly referred to as "ranchland" in the annual reports of the Department of the Interior because it was too dry for nineteenth century farming, and this allowed the rest of the west to retain its "good farmland" label.

Having thus made it easier for individuals to acquire larger blocks of western land, in the 1880s both governments began to worry about limiting the amount of land non-native individuals could control. It was a bigger concern for the United States because the nation was coming to the end of its "unlimited" western spaces, and those spaces were supposed to safeguard American democracy. The nation had long since reached the end of its continental territorial expansion; if the yeoman ideal was to survive, private individuals could not be permitted to possess particularly large land holdings, whether those holdings had been legally expanded through the Desert Lands Act or illegally acquired through some fast fencing. Canada, on the other hand, still felt it had some room to manoeuvre because it was not yet being swamped with immigrants, and it had never tied its national identity or destiny to the yeoman ideal. Even Canadian officials, however, felt that the time had come to start policing homesteaders more closely to ensure that the provisions of the Dominion Lands Act were being met and that no one was holding land unfairly. And by the mid-1880s, just a few short years after instituting the ranch lease system, the government even began putting more and more restrictions on the enormously profitable ranch leases to ensure that the door remained open for agricultural settlement in southern Alberta.[18]

In their efforts to establish and consolidate national hegemony over their western domains, the Canadian and American governments struggled to ensure that their maps of western lands and the policies they used to administer those lands accorded with the political, economic, and social maps they imagined for the region's future. By 1880 the forty-ninth parallel dividing Blackfoot country been surveyed and marked, and the land on either side of it was beginning to take on a clear shape and national purpose in the eyes of "its" respective government.

And yet, the land east of the Rockies always resisted Ottawa and Washington's efforts at categorizing and exploiting it. The relative lack of water meant that the region was better suited for large-scale stock-raising than small-scale agriculture and family farms. A border determined by astronomy meant that the line never manifested a physical existence beyond the widely separated cairns. And, just as the land itself refused to accord with national visions, the Blackfoot confederacy that straddled the border also refused to play along. Those wide-open spaces, of which these governments were so proud, still contained highly mobile indigenous communities who refused to respect things like imaginary national borders.

Both governments tried to subdue, contain, and reshape the Blackfoot in line with the ways they sought to control and re-vision the land. Their persistent transnational mobility created a cross-border problem, challenging the border at the same time as it lent greater meaning to the line. By constructing the mobility and large territories of plains peoples as their most essential characteristic, the governments defined their first goal: nothing else could be done with tribes like the Blackfoot until their mobility was eliminated and territory was reduced. "Indians" couldn't be "civilized" until they held still, preferably on a farm to speed up the assimilation process, and white farmers couldn't flock westward if native peoples were still free to move around – objectives that were clearly two sides of the same coin.

Even as the governments worked to reduce the mobility of and amount of territory occupied by native peoples within their borders, they continued to be frustrated by the Blackfoot's traditional and easy movement back and forth across the border between Alberta and Montana. The American officials seem to have found this more irritating than the Canadians, particularly during the 1870s when Canada had yet to conclude a treaty with the Blackfoot. In 1870 Lt. Col. Alfred Sully wrote from Montana that although the Blackfoot nation was "one of the largest nations of Indians at present in our country," they "do not all properly belong to the United States." Instead, "they claim in common a section of the country from the British line south some miles to the city of Helena, and north of the line to the Saskatchewan River. Being a wild, uncivilized set, they of course do not take into consideration any treaties we have with Great Britain in regard to our boundary line, but look upon the whole of the country both north and south of the line as theirs."[19] Officials noted that while the Blackfoot might not pay any attention to the invisible borders created by the whites, they did have their own. Agent J. Armitage wrote in 1871 that the Blackfoot seemed "to be governed by imaginary boundary-lines, and express themselves as perfectly willing to remain in what they consider their own country."[20]

Nevertheless, local and national officials wanted their own clear boundaries to take precedence and have meaning in Blackfoot country. In 1873 Montana agent William Ensign informed his superiors that while the Peigan came to the agency on a regular basis, his efforts to induce the Blackfoot and Blood had proved futile thus far. They ranged "north of the British line, from two hundred and fifty to four hundred miles from the agency, and are kept from coming in by illicit traders...." He was sure that the recent executive order setting out a reservation for the Blackfoot was going to be "of incalculable importance and benefit to the Indians and to the Department. Heretofore, with no defined reservation limits, a great portion of the work of the agent has necessarily proved futile in its results.... This laudable change will at once work radical cures for a great many existing evils."[21] He never specified precisely why or how "defined reservation limits" were going to cure the evils of the Blackfoot and their agents; it was simply taken for granted that they would.

The January 1870 attack by the United States Army on a Piikuni camp on the Marias River, during which 173 men, women, and children were killed, was the most extreme step the United States took in its efforts to tame the Blackfoot. Commissioner of Indian Affairs Ely Parker insisted that the ends justified the means, stating in his report on the massacre that "the killing of the women and children was accidental or unavoidable. Although the consequences were deplorable, yet they were effectual in completely subduing the Indians, and the entire nation has since not only been quiet, but even solicitous to enter into arrangements for permanent peace and good behaviour in the future."[22] Only briefly did any of the reports mention that this massacre had coincided with a smallpox epidemic, and it was likely the combined blows which led to the Piikuni's more sedentary and "solicitous" behaviour.

North American bureaucrats and would-be colonizers believed quite strongly that the indigenous population was occupying more than their fair share of the continent. Secretary of the Interior Columbus Delano stated in 1872 that the reservation system "withdraws the great body of Indians from the direct path of industrial progress, and allows the work of settlement and the extension of our railways to go forward up to the full limit of the capacities of capital and immigration...." He insisted that "little progress can be made in the work of civilization while the Indians are suffered to roam at large over immense reservations."[23] Restricting the mobility and range of Aboriginal communities was seen as serving two functions: it would make it easier for the whites to assimilate them, and it would be easier for the whites to settle and develop native lands.

Two years later Delano went so far as to suggest that full homesteading privileges should be extended to individual Indians, because "requiring a residence in the same place for five years" would "correct the roving instinct," although this suggestion was never actually implemented because of prevailing assumptions that Indians were not yet advanced enough as a race for "real" homesteading.[24] The fact that Canadian and American homestead legislation was never extended to Aboriginal communities indicates that, in spite of official rhetoric about assimilation through agriculture, the line between a white farmer and a native farmer was to remain clearly drawn.

While each government waited for reservations and railroads to solve their problems with indigenous communities, their favoured strategy was supervision. The most striking characteristic of the reports from the 1870s is an obsession with supervision, counting, and containment. Every year officials on both sides of the border stressed their continuing efforts to achieve statistical accuracy and thoroughness. But it wasn't easy: those immense spaces which were such a selling-point for attracting white settlers were the chief obstacle in the path of agents charged with overseeing their native wards. In his 1873 report Secretary Delano felt compelled to remind his readers that, whereas before the government could just relocate Aboriginal communities "into a country remote from civilization," it now had to preserve "order and security between the Indians and whites through a vast region of country, not less than four thousand miles in length by two thousand five hundred in width, extending from the extreme northern and northwestern limits of Washington Territory to the Gulf of Mexico, and from the line which separates the United States from the British possessions in the North to the line which separates the United States from the territory of Mexico in the extreme southwest."[25]

A similar complaint was registered in 1878 by David Laird, now Lieutenant-Governor of the North-West Territories. He stated that it was "impossible" to fill in all the blanks in the "tabular statement" the Department had sent to him to complete: "It cannot be expected that a Superintendent assisted by two agents whose time, since they entered on their duties in August last, has been taken up entirely in paying the Indians their annuities, could furnish a statement, for instance, of the number of fish caught or quantity of furs taken, or the number of shanties and wigwams, or the bushels of grain raised in a district extending from the boundary line of the United States to the Arctic Ocean, and from Keewatin and Manitoba to British Columbia and Alaska."[26] Although Laird was more concerned with tracking production and Delano with preserving the peace, their shared nemesis was the size of their domains.

Local agents kept trying, though. In 1874 Montana's Blackfoot Agent R. F. May reported that his efforts to "ascertain the number of souls comprising the three tribes" were not progressing as quickly or thoroughly as he would like. He said he had "no reliable information" about the Blackfoot and Blood because they still spent most of their time north of the line. He was "led to believe ... that they do not number over fifteen hundred each, though some accounts place the numbers much higher." His most ambitious project was to try and compile a census of the Indians who were "entitled to draw rations – with the intention of forwarding the same to your office when completed, but find it slow and tedious. Many of the Indians are averse to giving their names, and in many cases they have not named their younger children. To meet this difficulty I avail myself of the ingenuity of the interpreter ... in assisting the parents in naming them." He estimated it would take four to six more months to complete the census.[27]

A similar challenge was faced in southern Alberta in the 1880s as the Canadian government tried to compile accurate lists of who should be receiving treaty payments. In 1882 Agent Cecil Denny hired David Mills, whose mother was Kainah and father was African-American, to assist with the project. According to Blackfoot oral tradition, one of Mills's first tasks was to eliminate Piikuni from Montana who were trying to pass as Kainah in Alberta in order to collect both sets of treaty payments. His "ability to remember and classify the names of individuals and sizes of families played an important part in stopping the Bloods from trying to falsify their numbers to receive greater rations."[28]

These examples neatly capture the difficulties the two governments had in trying to control Blackfoot country during its uneven transition to the Montana-Alberta borderlands. The open spaces and original inhabitants of the land east of the Rockies were resisting attempts to divide up and portion out the land to the sort of resident who would have a name and hold still – white male farmers and ranchers. But even after this range of colonizing tools was supposed to have contained and remade the Blackfoot, white officials were still struggling to keep the lines drawn between whites and natives and were a long way from achieving their "civilizing" mission. The federal governments' key containment strategies proved insufficient in Blackfoot country, at least in part because of the tribes' transnational mobility, leaving white officials scrambling to achieve more complete control over the spatial and racial boundaries. Officials had to find more effective ways to change what happened behind the lines. Western peoples, like western lands, had to be bounded by lines that everyone could "see" and in theory agree upon. Then, to make those lines mean the right things, officials had to influence what happened on the "other" side by immobilizing and thus reshaping the economic, cultural, and gender norms of Blackfoot men and women.

Regulating the spatial limits of Aboriginal mobility was connected at a fundamental level with a desire to regulate every aspect of the social and racial boundaries. Late nineteenth-century whites wanted to believe in the utter separateness of "the races," but it is striking to note that American officials seemed to care more about white men intruding on the reserves, "degrading" themselves and their race by "going native," while the Canadians got more upset by Indian women heading into white towns for the purposes of prostitution. Canada's Indian Act ensured that an Aboriginal woman who married a white man was no longer legally considered an "Indian" and had to leave the reserve anyway. Because of these different national constructions of racialized masculinity and the threats posed by interracial mobility, the phrase "squaw man" had different implications depending on which side of the border that man was on.

Whites and natives were supposed to be and stay two distinct races, a supposedly self-evident truth that nevertheless had to be enforced by trying to keep Indians on Indian land and whites on white land. "Squaw men" and Aboriginal women's assumed prostitution symbolized the problems that ensued when spatial and racial boundaries were too porous and thus too easily thrown into question. It was taken for granted by white authorities that Aboriginal women who went to Calgary or Lethbridge to earn money through prostitution were degrading themselves, but more importantly they were degrading any whites they came into contact with. White men who married or lived on reserves with native women were thought to be degrading themselves (and by extension white masculinity) and were perceived as a dangerous source of discontent on the reserves.[29] Numerous measures were taken by white officials to create and enforce a racial and spatial buffer zone between natives and whites.

Of the five nations who had signed Treaty No. 7 in 1877, the Sarcee or Tsuu Tina were seen as the most problematic when it came to prostitution because of their proximity to Calgary. Among the three Blackfoot nations, however, the Kainah reserve's location near Lethbridge was seen as creating similar problems. In the late 1880s the Kainah band led by Calf Shirt had moved to the north end of the reserve, which was closest to the small town of Lethbridge. Their location "made it easy for female members of the tribe to slip into town in the evening, or for whites to come out.... To combat the problem, Calf Shirt was appointed a scout for the North-West Mounted Police. During the time he held this position, he fought to keep the undesirables out of his camp and succeeded to some extent in stamping out prostitution."[30] In this instance it was not the mobility of Aboriginal men that was causing problems for white officials; it was the mobility of Aboriginal women that had to be stopped, and male native leaders seemed willing to work with white officials to do so.

Secretary of the Interior Lamar wrote in his 1885 report that his department was determined to "suppress" the "great evils arising from the presence of bad and vicious white men within the reservations." A particular target were "'squaw men,' who marry or act as husbands with Indian women. The evil influence of these squaw men is said to be very great." They were said to "foment discord among the Indians themselves, disturb their peaceful inclinations towards the settlers in the country surrounding the reservation, and incite opposition on the part of the Indians to the measures adopted and regulations prescribed by the Department for their advancement and civilization." Lamar called for legislation that would force any Indian woman who married a white man to be "deemed a citizen" and ineligible to live on the reservation, similar to naturalization legislation that gave a woman the nationality of her husband. Lamar concluded that there "should be no exception to the law which makes the wife and children follow the state and condition of the father in favor of men whose low instincts make them abandon civilization and hide themselves from the restraints of law and free themselves from social ordinances and observances."[31] Although he does not mention Canada's Indian Act, it is striking to note that he is recommending the United States pursue identical legislation.

At the same time as the Blackfoot challenged the meaningfulness of the border by continuing to move back and forth across it, their mobility actually became a way for white officials to reinforce it. The Americans continued to refer to Canada as "the British possessions," for example, and each side blamed the whisky trade and horse raids on the other. In 1871, for example, the agent in Montana, J. Armitage wrote that as the "British lines" were only "seventy miles north of the agency and one hundred miles from Fort Benton, the whisky traders are afforded a safe harbor should they be pursued...."[32] In 1874 Montana Agent Robert May reported that it was taking longer than expected to get an accurate head count of the three tribes his agency was responsible for. He had "no reliable information" about the Blackfoot and Blood because they still spent most of their time north of the line, although he did think that their numbers had been greatly reduced over the previous four or five years: "The unrestricted intercourse they have enjoyed, on British soil, with the worst and most reckless class of white men on earth, has brought its attendant evils – whisky, powder and ball, disease and death." [33] The following year Canada's Department of the Interior was pleased to report that the Mounties had cleared southern Alberta of the "bands of outlaws and desperadoes from Montana and the neighbouring territories" who were supplying liquor and guns to the Blackfeet and other Indians.[34]

By the end of the 1870s both governments believed they had overcome or were very close to overcoming their first two problems with their western spaces: the land had been controlled through mapping, surveying and land laws, and the Aboriginal population was soon to be controlled through their physical marginalization and containment on the reserves. The land could therefore now be seen as properly and safely "empty," awaiting the tide of white immigrants, preferably men, who would claim and develop their 160-acre farms and add to the wealth of eastern governments.

The United States knew it did not have to exert itself to attract immigrants because it was already attracting the bulk of the world's migrants. Between

1861 and 1880 just over five million immigrants came to the United States, more than 4.3 million from Europe and over 537,000 from Canada and Newfoundland.[35] By comparison, the total immigration to Canada between 1867 and 1892 was about 1.5 million, although many of these were only passing through on their way to the United States.[36] Numbers like these allowed Joseph Wilson, Commissioner of the General Land Office, to declare bluntly in 1870 that the "United States is the favorite land of the emigrant. Other countries present equal attractions in the natural advantages of soil, climate, and position, but have never yet attracted immigration." Canada, for example, "lies in much closer proximity to Europe, offering advantages for settlement to its northern races, perhaps, equal to those of some of our Northwestern States, but in spite of every effort of the British Government, the large majority of the immigrants directed to this point are soon attracted to the more genial nationality of the United States of America."[37] Partly as a result of this confidence and partly as a result of the constitutional limits on federal involvement in immigration, the American government did little more than try to get accurate head counts of all the newcomers and worry about the conditions on board immigration ships.[38]

Although American federal officials talked very little about immigration when compared with the way the topic dominated Canadian discussions, most of what they did say was framed in terms of their goals for Western settlement – both as the key magnet for so many immigrants and as the main reason why the United States should try to get only the very best quality of newcomers. As Wilson stated in his 1870 report; "The masses of Europe and the settled populations of our own older States are especially interested in the grand openings to individual enterprise now developing in the Great West." He believed that "the homestead privilege" was going to act as an "incentive to a still more rapid movement of immigration."[39] Whatever the reason, the United States was receiving hundreds of thousands more newcomers than Canada every year.

Canada's federal government had the authority to take an active role in attracting immigrants, however, and when it came to the North-West Territories the government had a very clear idea of the kind of settlers it wanted. Spatial and racial concerns were in the forefront of the reports of agents and ministers alike. The government's main goal was to attract white male farmers, but even the preferred groups of white immigrants, such as the British,

Scottish, Scandinavians, Swiss, and Euro-Americans, were ranked according to their assumed ability to cope with the size of Canada's western lands. Many Europeans were dismissed for being, in effect, too small-scale: fine for growing "a slip of geranium in an earthen vessel" or feeding "a whole family on a few acres of ground," but hardly suited for large land grants.[40] Euro-American immigrants were greatly desired both for their assumed experience with frontier agriculture and settlement, and to try and demonstrate that Canada could attract Americans just as well as the United States seemed to be attracting the immigrants of the world.

Aboriginal and white women do not appear to have ever occupied anything other than a peripheral place in the United States' vision of what its West should look like,[41] but Canada's active Métis population and its efforts to attract white settlers forced the government to actively consider the "problems" caused by Aboriginal women and the resulting "need" for white women to settle the Northwest. The United States knew that it could do nothing and still get the majority of the world's migrants, and so put little thought into either immigration or tempering the masculinity of their West. It is clear that both governments took maleness for granted as much as whiteness as a key characteristic of desirable immigration, because ranching and large-scale agriculture, hardiness and rugged self-reliance were all associated with masculinity. But Canada's efforts to attract immigrants meant that it had to think about also attracting white women.

The most consistent and explicit role white women played in the Canadian state's view of immigration was as domestic servants, and every year the Canadian-based agents would plead for more young single women to come. Domestic servants and agricultural labourers were the two groups regularly given assisted passages. Only rarely did the agents make an explicit connection between encouraging more white women to come to Canada and providing wives for white men to keep the men from seeking partners among Aboriginal women. In 1879 Agent William Grahame, stationed in Minnesota, noted that if more white women did not come to Canada, the only other option for single male homesteaders would be "to lead a bachelor's life, or inter-marry with the Indian women...."[42] In 1886 the agent at Brandon, Manitoba wrote that more of an effort should "be made to send out strong, healthy young girls or women, accustomed to house work, to this country." Not only were they guaranteed to find work at a good wage, "their presence here would, there is not a doubt, ultimately lead to their filling more important positions, as the wives of the many young farmers who are now suffering the miseries and inconveniences of batchelorhood, on their prairie farms in Manitoba and the North-West." [43] Intermarriage was not a favoured containment technique in Canada because such unions led to "troublesome" Métis offspring.

When they weren't talking about white women coming to Canada as domestic servants, the immigration agents' reports usually cast white women in the roles of the reluctant emigrant and even more reluctant homesteader. In 1879, for example, the agent in Carlisle, England was pressuring the Canadian government to set aside land for a group colony from British border counties, in the same way that land had been reserved for group settlements of Mennonites and Icelanders. He used women's fears as one of his justifications: "One of the greatest fears among many of the best classes for settlers in this country, and especially among females, is that they would get into a new and wild country where they would know nobody, and that the people of the country would not be inclined to be friendly to them."[44] His message was that Canada could get more of the "best classes" of immigrants from England if the government would allow them to settle as a group and therefore provide familiarity and safety for the women.

The following year Agent William Grahame used women's delicacy as one of the rationales why men should emigrate to Canada ahead of their families. During a visit to Emerson, Manitoba he had been "struck" by "the disappointed look that was plainly visible on the faces of many of the new arrivals, especially the female portion of them. And indeed it was not to be wondered at, when we think of these people leaving comfortable homes in a country where everything was in an advanced state of improvement, and then imagine them on their arrival in this 'promised land,' their first step from the platform at the railway car being almost knee deep into mud." He thought that a man should arrive in the West in the fall so that when his family arrived in the spring he would already be prepared.[45]

Nevertheless, even these few remarks dramatically outnumber the references to women in the admittedly limited American discussions of immigration. Secretary of the Interior J. D. Cox remarked in 1870 that although one-fifth of the annual immigrants were younger than fifteen, "this deficiency is more than compensated for by the immense preponderance of the males over the females."[46] Two years later, during the discussion over proposed legislation to protect immigrants, the poor conditions on board ships from Europe were framed as posing particular dangers to the chastity of female passengers.[47] Whereas Canada saw white women as having at least some kind of role to play in colonizing western lands, the United States saw only liabilities in need of special protection.

By the end of the 1880s, then, not only had the forty-ninth parallel dividing Blackfoot country been surveyed and marked, but also the land on either side of it was beginning to take shape in the eyes of "its" respective government. The land was a little less far away and foreign, and the Blackfoot seemed less mobile and threatening than they had at the start of the decade. To achieve what they wanted to achieve in the West, Canada and the United States had to draw lines that mattered: the forty-ninth parallel had to clearly distinguish one country from the other, for example, and reservation boundaries were supposed to clearly separate "Indians" from whites.

As anything other than bureaucratic fictions, however, neither the racial nor spatial demarcations were progressing quickly or concretely. The transition from Blackfoot country to borderland was uneven and less than successful because eastern ideals and policies were never able to match up with western realities. Western land and its Aboriginal inhabitants resisted, and the discursive and policy grid of spatial, racial, and gendered assumptions had plenty of gaps. Nevertheless, both governments did make great strides towards their national goals of a settled, agricultural West, and by 1900 the lines and categories of the Alberta-Montana borderlands dominated what had been Blackfoot country.

NOTES

1   Studies that examine both sides of the Canada-U.S. border are not new, and include such classic works as Paul Sharp's *Whoop-Up Country*, Hana Samek's *The Blackfoot Confederacy 1880–1920: A Comparative Study of Canadian and U.S. Indian Policy* (Albuquerque: University of New Mexico Press, 1987) and Bennett and Kohl's *Settling the Canadian-American.* Works which employ a more explicitly comparative "borderlands" approach (by studying the border as a social construction and not as a political given) include the collection edited by Victor Konrad, *Borderlands: Essays in Canadian-American Relations* (Toronto: ECW Press, 1991); *Cowboys, Ranchers and the Cattle Business: Cross-Border Perspectives on Ranching History,* edited by Simon Evans, Sarah Carter, and Bill Yeo (Calgary, AB, and Boulder, CO: University of Calgary Press and University Press of Colorado, 2000); and Beth LaDow, *The Medicine Line.* The most exciting borderlands work can be found in such unpublished theses as David McCrady's "Living With Strangers: The Nineteenth-Century Sioux and the Canadian-American Borderlands" (Ph. D. thesis, University of Manitoba, 1998); Molly Rozum's "Grasslands Grown: A Twentieth-Century Sense of Place on North America's Northern Prairies and Plains" (Ph.D. Thesis, University of North Carolina at Chapel Hill, 2001); and Michel Hogue's "Crossing the Line: The Plains Cree in the Canada-United States Borderlands, 1870–1900" (M.A. Thesis, University of Calgary, 2002).

2   Benedict Anderson. *Imagined Communities: Reflections on the Origin and Spread of Nationalism.* (1st ed. 1983; Rev. ed. London: Verso, 1991), 184.

3   United States, Department of the Interior, *Report of the Secretary of the Interior.* House of Representatives Executive Document #1, Part 4. 41st Congress, 3rd session. October 31, 1870.

4   Canada, Department of the Interior, *Annual Report of the Deputy Minister*, Sessional Papers, Volume 7, #12, February 29, 1884.

5   United States, Department of the Interior, *Report of the Commissioner of the General Land Office.* 1867.

6   United States, Department of the Interior, *Report of the Commissioner of the General Land Office.* House Executive Documents, #1, Part 4, 41st Congress, 3rd session.

7   United States, Department of the Interior, *Report of the Commissioner of the General Land Office.* House of Representatives Executive Document #1. 42nd Congress. 1871.

8   United States, Department of the Interior, *Report of the Surveyor-General of Montana.* House of Representatives Executive Document #1, Part 5. 42nd Congress, 3rd session. 1872.

9   United States, Department of the Interior, *Report of the Surveyor-General of Montana.* House of Representatives Executive Document #1, Part 5, 43rd congress, 2nd session. 1874.

10 Canada, Department of the Interior, *Report of Surveyor General* Sessional Papers 1884, Vol. 7, #12. 31st December 1883.

11   Canada, Department of the Interior, *Annual Report of the Department of the Interior for year ending 30th June 1874*. Sessional Papers 1875.

12   Richard White, *"It's Your Misfortune and None of My Own": A History of the American West*. (Norman: University of Oklahoma Press, 1991), 142.

13   Everett Dick, *The Lure of the Land: A Social History of the Public Lands from the Articles of Confederation to the New Deal*. (Lincoln: University of Nebraska Press, 1970), 158.

14   United States. Department of the Interior. *Report of the Commissioner of the General Land Office*, 1867.

15   Canada, Department of the Interior, *Annual Report of the Department of the Interior for year ending 30th June 1875*, Sessional Papers 1876, #9.

16   Canada, *An Act to amend the Dominion Lands Act*, 1876. Section 4.

17   United States, Department of the Interior, *Report of Commissioner of General Land Office*, House Executive Documents #1, Part 5, 44th Congress, 1st Session, October 28, 1875.

18   It is clear that American officials anticipated Frederick Jackson Turner's famous 1892 declaration about the end of the frontier by several years, while Canadian officials clung to their faith in their "last best west" until the turn of the century. Turner, "The Significance of the Frontier in American History." *Frontier and Section: Selected Essays of Frederick Jackson Turner*. For a discussion of the late-nineteenth perception of Canada's prairies as the "last best west" see Doug Owram's *Promise of Eden*.

19   United States, Department of the Interior, *Report of Lt-Col. Alfred Sully, Montana Superintendancy*, House of Representatives Executive Document #1, Part 4. 41st congress, 3rd session. 1870.

20   Ibid., *Report of Blackfoot Indian Agent J. Armitage*, House of Representatives Executive Document #1. 42nd Congress. 1871.

21   Ibid., *Report of Blackfoot Agent William T. Ensign*, House of Representatives Executive Document #1, Part 5. 43rd Congress, 1st session. October 31, 1873.

22   Ibid., *Report of the Commissioner of Indian Affairs*, House of Representatives Executive Document #1, Part 4. 41st Congress, 3rd session. October 31, 1870.

23   United States, Department of the Interior, *Report of the Secretary of the Interior*, House of Representatives Executive Document #1, Part 5, 42nd Congress, 3rd session. October 31, 1872.

24   United States, Department of the Interior, *Report of the Secretary of the Interior*, House of Representatives Executive Document, #1, Part 5, 43rd congress, 2nd session. 1874.

25   Ibid., 1st session. October 31, 1873.

26   Canada, Department of the Interior, *Annual Report of the Department of the Interior*, Sessional Papers 1878, #10.

27   United States, Department of the Interior, *Report of the Blackfoot Indian Agent R. F. May*, House of Representatives Executive Document #1, Part 5, 43rd congress, 2nd session, September 10, 1874.

28   "Black White Man" *in The Amazing Death of Calf Shirt and Other Blackfoot Stories: Three Hundred Years of Blackfoot History*, collected by Hugh A. Dempsey (Saskatoon, SK: Fifth House, 1994) 98.

29   Prostitution was not mentioned at all by Blackfoot agents in Montana, perhaps because the reserve wasn't close enough to any sizeable white settlements and perhaps because their real concern was the denigration of white masculinity.

30   "The Snake Man," in *The Amazing Death of Calf Shirt and Other Stories*, 147.

31   United States, Department of the Interior, *Annual Report of the Secretary of the Interior*, House Executive Documents, 49th Congress 1st Session, Document #1, Part 5. November 1, 1885.

32   United States, Department of the Interior, *Report of Blackfoot Indian Agent J. Armitage*, 1871.

33   Ibid., *Report of Blackfoot Indian Agent R. F. May*, House of Representatives Executive Document #1, Part 5, 43rd congress, 2nd session, September 10, 1874.

34   Canada, Department of the Interior, *Annual Report of the Department of the Interior for 1875*, Sessional Papers 1876.

35   United States, Department of Justice, Immigration and Naturalization Service, *Report of the Select Commission on Western Hemisphere Immigration*. January 1968.

36   Ninette Kelley and Michael Trebilcock, *The Making of the Mosaic: A History of Canadian Immigration Policy* (Toronto: University of Toronto Press, 1998), 63.

37   United States, Department of the Interior, *Report of the Commissioner of the General Land Office*, House of Representatives Executive Document #1, Part 4, 41st Congress, 3rd session, October 31, 1870.

38   The United States had a National Bureau of Immigration from 1864–1868, but it died because of inefficiency and state-rights concerns and there was relatively little direct federal involvement until the Immigration and Naturalization Service was created in the early 1890s.

39   United States, Department of the Interior, *Report of the Commissioner of the General Land Office*, House Executive Documents #1, Part 4, 41st Congress, 3rd session, October 31, 1870.

40   The first comment came from the agent in London (Canada, Department of Agriculture, *Report of Minister of Agriculture for 1870*, Sessional Papers 1871, #64), while the second is from European Agent Edward Barnard Jr. (Canada, Department of Agriculture, *Annual Report of Minister of Agriculture for 1872*, Sessional Papers 1873, #26).

41   Aboriginal women do not appear to have been mentioned at all in the American reports of the 1870s except for those who were killed or captured during the Marias massacre.

42   Canada, Department of Agriculture, *Report of the Minister of Agriculture*, Sessional Papers 1879, #9.

43   Ibid., *Report by Brandon Manitoba Agent*, Sessional Papers 1886, Volume #7, Paper #10.

44   Ibid., *Report of the Minister of Agriculture*, Sessional Papers 1879, #9.

45 Ibid., *Report of Immigration Agent at Duluth Minnesota*, Sessional Papers 1880. Volume #7. S. P. #10.

46 United States, Department of the Interior, *Report of the Secretary of the Interior*, House of Representatives Executive Document #1, Part 4. 41st Congress, 3rd session. October 31, 1870.

47 United States, Senate, *Message from the President recommending Legislation in relation to the transportation of immigrants to and within the United States*, Senate Executive Document #73, 42nd Congress, 2nd session.

Chapter 7

"The Spark that Jumped the Gap": North America's Northern Plains and the Experience of Place[1]

Molly P. Rozum, Doane College

"Is it desirable to ignore the International Boundary when discussing the Northern Plains?"[2] Carl Kraenzel of Montana and Watson Thompson of Manitoba asked this question in 1942 of residents of North America's northern grasslands, from South Dakota to Saskatchewan. Their inquiry grew out of the North American Regionalization Project sponsored by the Rockefeller Foundation (RF) in New York. This essay explores transnational regional identity through the Canadian and American participants of – what the foundation labelled – the "Northern Plains" inquiry. The region they defined included the southern areas of the Canadian provinces of Alberta, Saskatchewan, and Manitoba and the states of North Dakota, South Dakota, and Nebraska, and parts of Minnesota, Montana, Wyoming, and Colorado. In 1942, the Rockefeller Foundation sponsored three conferences, one each in New York City, Lincoln, Nebraska, and Saskatoon, Saskatchewan. From Canadian and American leaders, the RF hoped to hear a "plains sensibility" defined in North American terms. The conferences' official transcripts offer rare glimpses into people addressing regional identity directly.[3]

After considering conference attendees' ideas about a Canada-U.S. plains connection, other voices from the Prairies and Plains are considered for the light they shed on the problem of transnational regional unity in the 1940s. And unity was a problem. The conference series left the existence of a Northern Plains regional transnational unity unresolved. Unity was something definitely felt, but ineffable and elusive in terms of concrete institutional expression. The additional voices examined in the second half of the essay recall day-to-day living in various North American grasslands communities, and suggest the substance of what RF participants could not quite articulate. A sensuous relationship with a wild and commercial grasslands habitat and personal histories grafted on to the region's landscape encouraged transnational connection.

World War II instigated the Rockefeller Foundation's 1940s regionalization project. When the war interrupted the New York foundation's world-centred projects, officials of the Humanities Section looked home to North America, defining the continent as a "neglected" world region.[4] Director David H. Stevens and John Marshall, associate director, explained the new inquiry as "fresh scrutiny in order to gain right recognition" of the "worn" phrase "'the American tradition.'" They wished to give voice to a *continental* perspective. From conferences, the RF hoped to hear "soundings" of regional "outlooks" that would reveal "the human imprint of the environment."[5] Foundation officers speculated about the project's great potential. Regionalism, they explained, "may have much to do with internationalism by making men of every race realize the special possessions of individuals and groups by virtue of their regional origins."[6] Several questions guided them: "What do North Americans now think about themselves? What do they feel that they belong to? What are they conscious of – What is in their minds?"[7]

Initially, the foundation planned to hold international North American conferences focused on all areas of the U.S.-Canadian-Mexican borderlands. After canvassing the continental borders by interviewing regional experts individually, it became "clear" to the foundation operatives "that the Plains area had a lot of special values and had a lot of specialists" already working to answer questions of regional outlook.[8] Forays into other North American regions showed the RF mandate to be "so novel" that Stevens and Marshall predicted any project would become a "several year" process, even to start asking the appropriate questions. "The evident exception," they sold regionalization to foundation trustees, "was the N[orthern] P[lains] w[h]ere people were almost ready to move as of themselves."⁹ The Rockefeller inquiry into the Plains (and offshoots) lasted almost a decade. No other transborder region achieved more than an initial conference.¹⁰

What exactly led the male leadership of the Prairies and Plains to "move" on the issue of transnational regional unity? The foundation of course made it easy with generous funding. Who would turn down a wealthy foundation's interest in their home region – one, of late, maligned and dirtied by dust? Equally attractive were all-expenses-paid trips to New York City and week-end-stays in Lincoln's grand Hotel Cornhusker and Saskatoon's opulent Hotel Bessborough. An increased attention to life across the boundary, however, seemed to be a legacy of the 1930s degradation that this one continental region caused two separate nations. Dust spirals in a sense blotted out the international border and underscored a basic commonness that grasslands residents shared to the exclusion of their respective national cohorts.¹¹ But did a special international relationship really distinguish North America's northern grasslands?

The Northern Plains conferences led to no simple answers. At the first conference in New York, historian George Smith of Alberta struck the character of lasting general opinion. He felt the simultaneousness of "great similarities" and "great differences, as far as the borderline is concerned."¹² Minnesota historian Theodore C. Blegen believed "an emotional unity" developed out of "the emotional adjustment of people to the environment in which they live and to their neighbors."¹³ "The little things of nature" held the key to a common transnational regional identity, according to J. Frank Dobie, of the University of Texas. Mesquite, coyotes, and prickly-pear blossoms, the substance of the land, he thought, connected people – or could connect people.¹⁴ Walter Prescott Webb, by then already a famous historian of the Plains, believed the same. He did not question unity, but unity's latency. Webb thought a transnational popular magazine might "give some coherence to this whole region, emphasize a little of its unity, and ... knit the region together." "The flight of ducks and the life of the jackrabbit and prairie dogs" would be sources of "common interests between people in Canada and the southern Plains," he felt sure. "Take drought, for example," Webb spoke on. "Drought holds the same terror in Canada that it does in Texas; and there isn't anything about a state line that it respects."[15] For A. L. Burt, from the University of Minnesota, but with prior experience in Canadian education, "the spark that jumped the gap" was the Métis slow-carted buffalo robe trade of the 1830s and 1840s along the Red River road between St. Paul [Minnesota] and Fort Gary [Winnipeg, Manitoba]. From that historical moment, jumping the forty-ninth parallel, he said, "has ever since been continued."[16] These comments all show a certain goodwill deference to the idea of international regional connections.

Skepticism, however, laced the discussion. Oklahoma University professor Walter Stanley Campbell pinpointed the crux of the problem: "The Plains extend North and South, roughly; but the trails and the cultural currents are all East and West."[17] "If it hadn't been for that railway," Burt charged, "what is now the Canadian West would have been the backdoor of the American Revolution."[18] Later, W. M. Whitelaw, of the University of Saskatchewan, echoed this sentiment. The Canadian government, he said, "has control of the railways and ... have been willing to do uneconomic things ... for national interest."[19] A general consensus emerged around an economic-political interpretation of the "gap" separating the United States and Canada. The "gap" holding a continuous ecological region apart might be jumped, but national governments, since the latter nineteenth century, had worked – through industry (particularly the powerful railroads), finance, and law – to widen the gap, rather than narrow it.[20] These had been conscious, economic nationalist choices.

Region, it must be concluded for these grasslands residents, did respect political lines – down to the most basic matter of travel. Whitelaw doubted whether he could easily travel to Montana from Saskatchewan, right then in the 1940s. George Smith agreed, citing Montana as "the region of least intercommunication between Canada and the United States."[21] (This is astonishing given the long history between Alberta and Montana cattlemen and the well-worn path between Fort Macleod and Fort Benton.)[22] Nevertheless, it appeared easier in the 1940s for Montanans and Saskatchewanians to travel to New York City than to each other's prominent cities. After the Saskatoon Plains conference, a young Montana scholar, Frederick Kraenzel, wrote to Stevens and Marshall in New York "to express my appreciation," explaining, "Many of us got into Canada for the first time. It was an education for me, especially the fact of getting north and south in a region where most things go east and west."[23]

The lack of a thriving transnational regional identity becomes evident when at the initial New York meeting Walter Prescott Webb, author of the landmark study *The Great Plains* (1931), admitted, "I think this is the first time I ever sat around a table with a group of Canadians.... I know of no other example where a group has got together, outside of the Department of Agriculture, to give any consideration at all to the unity of the Great Plains region."[24] Now Webb grew up on the Plains of Texas and had spent years researching, writing, and teaching grasslands history. The lack of attention Webb gave to the Canadian Prairie Provinces in his own work told on him. Canadians proved no better. Between the conferences in New York and Lincoln, Professor Whitelaw surveyed some of his colleagues and students at the University of Saskatchewan about Webb's striking 1931 environmental interpretation of the region. "They hadn't heard of it," he reported.[25]

The conference attendees never seemed to get past *feelings* of unity to clear articulation of the basis for perceiving the grasslands as a transnational region. George Ferguson, managing editor of the *Winnipeg Free Press*, tried to explain how the "area becomes part of ourselves and something distinctive, and yet we talk about it and can't put our fingers on it. We get sentimental about the Plains, all of us who love them. But you can't lay your hands on the body of tradition and the deep roots."[26] "Again," George Smith testified, "the Great Plains area, I feel, has a unity and that unity is something I can feel."[27] Historian J. D. Hicks concurred with an apologetic waver for a lack of supporting facts. But psychologically speaking, he advanced, "You can more or less see it in their eyes. These people have the idea of spaciousness, bigness for the continent, bigness of outlook which I don't associate with any other section that I have come into contact with so completely."[28] Even Whitelaw cheered of the "enthusiastic" reception Webb's Plains study received, after he had introduced it to colleagues and students. "They recognized the truth of it" for Saskatchewan, he spoke confidently.[29]

It is clear conference participants recognized an elemental shared culture flowing from environmental relationships. Hicks came the closest to articulating a distinct element when he argued for the role space played in the culture of the region. People organized space differently and held different spatial parameters. In and of itself, the RF cross-border conversations suggested a bond of connection. The Plains and Prairies shared a common beleaguered status within both Canada and the United States. The erosion of economic, social, and soil stability during the depression and drought of the 1930s energized the exchange among residents who believed discussion would strengthen their region, despite its location in two separate nations. The conferences turned out to be more about banding together across the border to find ways to strengthen a region that beguiled its residents, than about recording the unique characteristics of an international regional "outlook."

The Northern Plains as a continental, transnational region lacked *institutional* expression, not a shared cultural connection. The central task, for conference participants, if not the stated goal of RF officials, became how to implement such formal expression. Optimistically, some saw potential for increased connection through recent transportation advances. The prevalence and affordability of automobiles and trucks and increasing miles of paved highways might free residents from stationary railroad tracks, without falling back to actual horse-power speeds.[30] Kraenzel and Thompson viewed RF resources as an opportunity to start a widespread popular movement for regional planning, involving farm resettlement. The Tennessee Valley Authority in the American South served as a model. Webb clung to the idea of an intellectual region, with paper – a popular magazine – going the distance of space. Theodore Blegen pursued his idea that a regional press could serve as a conduit for channelling financial support to creative individuals whose ideas would make manifest the illusive regional "outlook."[31] The projects discussed at the conferences aimed at realizing what was felt to be a *latent* connection among transnational residents of the Northern Plains.

A deeper look into the lives of residents who grew up during the capitalist transformation of North America's grasslands, suggests what the Rockefeller Foundation discussants of the 1940s could not "put our fingers on," to borrow George Ferguson's phrase.[32] J. D. Hicks hit on part of the problem. It was difficult for historians and experts, who in their professional lives relied on what they considered to be concrete facts, to think of emotions as evidence.[33] Sensing reluctance on this very issue, Theodore Blegen had asked the conference attendees outright: "Why are historians so afraid of dealing with emotions?" "They are often hard to footnote," replied Hicks.[34] Though the RF invited them "not so much as scholars as lay, but articulate, representatives of a region, and of its people," director David Stevens noted the discomfort among participants on this point.

Many residents raised within the grasslands, or who felt deeply tied to the region no matter how long their residency, felt little compunction about expressing ties to place. The substance of emotional ties during this period came in large part from a high level of physical interaction with grasslands habitats. The relationship of wild to commercial grasses and the new ecological makeup of grazing lands set unique historical parameters for sensuous "experience" of the region in the late-nineteenth and the first half of the twentieth century.[35] In pre-World War II years, people's bodies touched the earth and the air more than they would later, after agriculture became fully mechanized. The human body became more protected and air more filtered over time. People's experience of the same region changes over time as ways of interacting with and absorbing its features change. An intimacy with grasslands environments, from lush prairie to dust dunes, shaped this generation's experiences of place in ways that were fundamentally inaccessible to latter prairie and plains generations. The experience of the former became preserved inheritance (in parks, ecological sanctuaries, and memoirs) for the latter.

The memoirs of Annora Brown, who grew up in Fort McLeod, Alberta at the turn of the twentieth century, begin to suggest the unifying substance in the environment that RF participants sensed important. She spent most of her childhood (and a considerable part of her adulthood) wandering outdoors. The bare-footed Brown played in the rock pile on the edge of town, walked on the prairie to search for flowers, and camped for weeks amidst the trees on nearby river bottoms. Writing in her elderly years, Brown noted explicitly how she could "still recall my sensations as a child." Changing smells signalled the seasons, from wild roses, wolf willow, and the scent of "hot sun on green leaves" in the summer to the "bitter smell of frosted leaves" on the approach of winter. She remembered the "weight" of hot atmosphere on her skin.[36] Similarly, Thorstina Jackson, who grew up in an Icelandic North Dakota community, remembered the "abundant wild fruit in the woods, such as raspberries, serviceberries, pin cherries and wild plums." Her favourite spot for berries was "near the corral where the *serviceberry* bushes grew to wondrous size."[37] (Her cohorts north of the forty-ninth parallel labelled these *Saskatoon* bushes.) The taste of berries and the smells and touches of plant growth suggest the force of the senses upon body and memory, or as Frank Dobie might have said, these are "the little things of nature" that conditioned environmental expectations. Such expectations might be "the special possessions," gifted to people "by virtue of their regional origins," about which RF officials speculated when they thought about the potential of regionalism.[38]

Geologic-atmospheric processes flowed unlimited by national borders creating further chances for connection based on common experience. Even in the most semi-arid locations glacial "pot holes" allowed tall prairie species the chance to root. Similarly, sun-baked hills hosted tufts of short grasses within tall grass prairies. Various "Badlands" existed, for the same environmental reasons, in Alberta, Saskatchewan, Montana, North Dakota, and South Dakota. Some version of titled wooded "hills" such as the Sweet Grass Hills, Turtle Mountains, Cypress Hills, Slim Buttes, and the Black Hills marked the mental maps of most grasslands residents. Such sites drew people to them for the same resources, for wood, coal, and entertainment. One young boy recalled helping his father dig coal in the Alberta badlands. His father also gathered wood from the Cypress Hills. The acts of boys and men digging coal and chopping wood was repeated many times over in similar resource habitats across the northern grasslands. The diaries of Elsie Hammond, a young woman raised on the Saskatchewan grasslands near Maple Creek, revealed French George's Butte and her local "Pine Hills" as destinations for pleasure walks and horseback outings.[39] Simultaneity of geology and ecology across a large space, common bodily, sensual experience of the place, and patterns of movement through space, all together, forged the potential for cultural connection within the bioregion.[40]

The mental connections created across geographic space by story and personal narrative suggest how *culture* works with landscape and ecology to build regions. Adults introduced children to certain features that the latter did not always encounter personally. Annora Brown liked to sit on her home's rooftop and stare at the sky. A trail meandered away from her between the "massive" Chief Mountain and the Belly Buttes. Where did the trail go? She must have queried her father. She knew that the "winding trail" led to Fort Benton, Montana, located on the Missouri River. Fort Benton served as the earliest supply centre to Canada's North-West Territories and played a large role in the growth of her hometown, Fort Macleod, Alberta. Both forts were central to her father's career as a mounted policeman. She recalled that her father's "reputation as an old timer" brought old friends to their home and "strangers who were themselves old-timers and who wanted someone to share their memories."[41] The view of a trail, then, simultaneously bound Annora to her father, his past experience, and to a transborder space. Brown grew personal roots all along that historic north-south trail through the culture of story – even if she did not much, if ever, traverse it. National division of the land only intersected her mind's eye view; it did not crop the view to a Canada-only scene. Rather, the inheritance of crossborder stories made that view panoramic across national spaces.

The annual rise of the north-flowing Red River and its frequent flooding drew into its orbit Thorstina Jackson. In an autobiographical portrait of her generation of North American Icelanders, Jackson remembered standing in the spring "tearfully" on the other side of the Tongue River from the schoolhouse. "The bridge" she needed was "completely out of sight, covered with surging waters."[42] Where does the river flow? Thorstina Jackson must have asked about the Tongue River. It met the north-flowing Red River, which continued past Winnipeg, Manitoba, until it emptied into Lake Winnipeg. The flow of the Red River through North Dakota to Manitoba would have underscored other cross-border connections active in Jackson's Icelandic community. Indeed, while her mother arrived in North Dakota by passing through western Minnesota, her father migrated south from Winnipeg, a cultural centre for Icelandic North Americans. Later, her father would move back to Canada. North Dakota Icelanders took one of two rival Winnipeg Icelandic-print newspapers to stay abreast of community trends. Reflecting this border straddling, Jackson attended primary and secondary school in North Dakota, and college in Winnipeg. Thorstina Jackson's embeddedness in one historic community, spreading across two nations, bound her to one grassland, but three nations: the United States, Canada, and Iceland.[43]

Story, topography, geology, and ecology provided residents of the continental grasslands the raw resources with which to make connections across a broad geographic space. For national conquest to succeed, however, the newly born-and-raised in territories gained by conquest also must be raised into conceptions of space and into connections between space and place and nation. Locality, sensuously known, also began at an early age to be abstracted into the larger entities of section, rural municipality, township, county, state, province, and nation. Abstraction provided sensuous experience with national frameworks that directed views inward and helped to determine the boundaries of personal experience. The map work of the eight-year-old Hale Humphrey provides a glimpse into how the process works. "I have drew the map of Faulk County and are drawing the map of Dakota," he explained in one of his boyhood correspondence enclosures.[44] On that county map survives pencilled dots for his town and nine others of comparable size, the winding course of the Nixon River (running near his family's homestead), and the grid of township sections. He squared the space without regard to topography or prior Aboriginal methods of organizing the region's space. Hale embedded his nation's conquest by naming and organizing space, according to his culture's mandates.

Saskatchewan resident Elsie Hammond did the same. She studied "Canadian History" in high school, and the "The Prairie Provinces" as a unit in Normal School.[45] If she had not already learned, she learned then the mapped boundaries of nation and region. The action of drawing maps in mind and on paper and teaching boundaries *naturalized* the land of Hale's Faulk county and a "Dakota" place and Hammond's region, "The Prairie Provinces" – the latter a distinctly Canadian label for North America's northernmost grasslands. The combination of a nationally abstracted learned place and a physically absorbed ecological habitat provides a glimpse of the origins of ambivalence felt by the Rockefeller Foundation conference participants as they debated transnational regional unity and division. The conferences represented an attempt to move beyond national constructs for locating individuals in space.

People's experiences with a "plains" environment had long encouraged them to think, though not necessarily to move, beyond national borders. This type of intellectual border crossing can be seen in the work of the multitalented Annora Brown. In 1954, Brown published a collection of original prairie flora drawings accompanied by multicultural essays on their lore.[46] A "purely Canadian book," one reviewer wrote of *Old Man's Garden*, "What is important is the . . . gossip that takes you back to the oldest Indian legends and forward through all the early explorers of the west, on both sides of the boundary." What was meant by "purely Canadian" is unclear, but the reference to "both sides of the boundary" suggests the reviewer may have meant purely North American or purely prairie – Canada in contrast to Great Britain or France, not in contrast to the United States. The book's commercial launching showed a conscious continental approach. Brown's publisher planned "to send review copies to the leading papers in Montana, Idaho, and North Dakota, and ... circulars to various people in these states. I have a feeling," he underlined the strategy, "that there should be a good market for your book in these portions of the U.S.A. We will do what we can to exploit it."[47]

When seed-breeder North Dakotan George Will wrote *Corn for the Northwest* (1930) he meant for his agricultural instruction to apply to "both the American and Canadian Northwest." In his effort to breed corn seeds for hardiness and short maturity he catered to the agricultural needs of "northern Minnesota, western South Dakota, most of Wyoming, Montana, North Dakota, and Manitoba, Saskatchewan, and Alberta in western Canada." Seeds with the quality to withstand drought and that ran the race against cold weather were essentials for Northern Plains agriculture, without regard to any political boundary. And the addresses of letters sent by satisfied customers to Will's store in Bismarck show that his base indeed lived throughout the binational area he defined in 1930 as the Northwest.[48]

George Will's book offered advice on how special varieties of corn could bring wild prairies and plains grasses under commercial control, while Annora Brown's book collected the legend and life associated with an Aboriginal organization of space that both she and Will knew intimately as children. What is significant here is that the environment, in both wild and tamed manifestations, encouraged people to think across the border. The Northern Plains inquiry constitutes one more example of an intellectual border crossing fostered by environmental concerns. Shared experiences with the land and atmosphere of the grasslands, at a point in history when people generally had close contact with the environment, created the "emotional unity" noted by Minnesotan Theodore Blegen and the "something distinctive" mentioned by Manitoban George Ferguson at the Rockefeller Foundation's conferences. In the sensuous realm of life, the people with whom Prairie and Plains residents would have the best chance of sharing such a regional sensibility would be other grasslands residents, from both sides of the forty-ninth parallel, regardless of their Canadian or U.S. citizenship. Not insignificant when one considers that the senses negotiate the spaces, landscapes, and built environments of day-to-day life. A sense of place proved to be, to use A.L. Burt's phrase, the "spark that jumped the gap" of the international boundary in the 1940s.

NOTES

1   I wish to acknowledge generous support for this research by way of a 1997 Canadian Studies Graduate Student Fellowship from the Canadian Embassy, Washington, D.C., and a 1999 Research Grant from the Rockefeller Archive Center, Sleepy Hollow, New York. For their time and comments, I also thank two anonymous reviewers for the University of Calgary Press and my friend and colleague Regina Sullivan for pointing me in some good directions.

2   Carl F. Kraenzel, Watson Thomson, and Glenn H. Craig, *The Northern Plains in a World of Change* (Canada [Winnipeg, MB]: Gregory-Cartwright, Ltd., October 1942), 65.

3   "Proceedings [of the] Conference on the Great Plains Area," Transcript, New York City, April 17–18, 1942, folder 3297, box 276; "Conference on the Northern Plains Transcript," Lincoln, Nebraska, June 25–27, 01942, folder 3299, box 277; and "Conference on the Northern Plains in a World of Change" Transcript, Saskatoon, SK, September 24–25, 1942, folder 3300, box 277, all series 200 R, Record Group 1.1, Rockefeller Foundation Archives, Rockefeller Archive Center, Sleepy Hollow, New York (hereafter RAC). The conferences began discussing the entire Great Plains, but quickly narrowed to the Northern Plains. Despite this emphasis, however, only one South Dakotan attended one of the conferences (at Saskatoon) and no one from North Dakota attended any of the conferences, although one North Dakotan was invited to the third conference. South Dakota later became one site for the RF's pilot adult study-group project.

4   David H. Stevens, "The Humanities Program of the Rockefeller Foundation: A Review of the Period, 1942–1947," 21 and 23, April 15, 1948, folder 14, box 2, series 911, Record Group 3, Rockefeller Foundation Archives, RAC.

5   [David H. Stevens? and/or John Marshall?], "A Review and Summaries of a Survey Covering Four Regions of North America, 1942," 1, folder 27, box 3, series 911, Record Group 3, Rockefeller Foundation Archives, RAC. "Outlook" is a term used throughout the foundation's regional studies documents.

6   David H. Stevens, "Review of Humanities Program, 1939–1941," 33, folder 13, box 2, series 911, Record Group 3, Rockefeller Foundation Archives, RAC.

7   David H. Stevens or John Marshall, untitled report, Dec. 10, 1942, 1, folder 25, box 3, series 911, Record Group 3, Rockefeller Foundation Archives, RAC.

8   New York Transcript, 2 (see n. 3).

9   "Regional Inquiry" memo between David H. Stevens and John Marshall, December 8, 1942, 1, folder 25, box 3, series 911, Record Group 3, Rockefeller Foundation Archives, RAC.

10   For a list of regional projects funded by the RF see Stevens, "The Humanities Program … Review … 1942–1947" (n. 4). Other regions received some RF funding for particular projects.

11   The problem of drought on the Plains surfaced frequently in the RF conference transcripts. See Walter P. Webb's comments, Lincoln Conference Transcript, 18 and

44; the content of Kraenzel, et. al., *Northern Plains*, (the study guide discussed in the third Saskatoon Conference Transcript); and Stevens, untitled report (n. 7), 3. See also Howard R. Lamar, "Comparing Depressions: The Great Plains and Canadian Prairie Experiences, 1929–1941," 175–206, In *The Twentieth-Century West*, Gerald D. Nash and Richard W. Etulain, eds. (Albuquerque: University of New Mexico Press, 1989); David C. Jones, *Empire of Dust* (Edmonton: University of Alberta Press, 1991); and Donald Worster, *Dust Bowl* (New York: Oxford University Press, 1979).

12 New York Transcript, 22.

13 Lincoln Transcript, 13.

14 Ibid., 88; and New York Transcript, 33–37.

15 Ibid., 81–82; New York Transcript, 69 and 71; and Walter P. Webb, *The Great Plains* (Boston: Ginn, 1931; reprint, Lincoln: University of Nebraska Press, 1981).

16 New York Transcript, 14–15.

17 Ibid., 23.

18 Ibid., 14–15.

19 Lincoln Transcript, 57–58.

20 See Alan Trachtenberg, *The Incorporation of America* (New York: Hill and Wang, 1982) and Doug Owram, *Promise of Eden*.

21 New York Transcript, 59.

22 Study of the Montana-Alberta connection has been the most active, suggesting a rich history of transborder movement. A classic is Sharp's *Whoop-Up Country* (Reprint, Helena: Historical Society of Montana, 1960). More recent studies include John W. Bennett and Seena B. Kohl, *Settling the Canadian-American West, 1890–1915* (Lincoln: University of Nebraska Press, 1995); and Beth LaDow, *The Medicine Line*.

23 Carl F. Kraenzel to John Marshall, November 2, 1942, folder 3143, box 262, series 200 R, Record Group 1.1, Rockefeller Foundation Archives, RAC. The sociologist Kraenzel went on to write a major synthesis of the U.S. Plains region, *The Great Plains in Transition* (Norman: University of Oklahoma Press, 1955). Surprisingly, the book demonstrates little analysis of the Canadian Prairie Provinces.

24 New York Transcript, 19 and 71.

25 Lincoln Transcript, 82.

26 New York Transcript, 38.

27 Lincoln Transcript, 28.

28 New York Transcript, 5.

29 Lincoln Transcript, 82.

30 Ibid., 50–51.

31 For a list of regional projects funded by the RF see note 4, and Kraenzel, et. al., note 2.

32 For the capitalist transformation of the countryside see Hal S. Barron, *Mixed Harvest* (Chapel Hill, NC: University of North Carolina Press, 1997) and Mary Neth, *Preserving the Family Farm* (Baltimore: Johns Hopkins University Press, 1995).

33   Widespread scholarly attention to the role of emotions in history and the history of emotions is of recent origin. See Peter N. Stearns and Jan Lewis, eds., *An Emotional History of the United States* (New York: New York University Press, 1998).

34   Lincoln Transcript, 23.

35   I have drawn on the following theorists for the significance of the effects of place on the body and mind: Yi-Fu Tuan, *Topophilia* (New Jersey: Prentice-Hall, 1974); Tuan, *Space and Place* (Minneapolis: University of Minnesota Press, 1977); Joan Scott, "The Evidence of Experience," *Critical Inquiry* 17 (summer 1991): 773–97; and Paul Rodoway, *Sensuous Geographies* (London: Routledge, 1994).

36   Annora Brown, *Sketches From Life* (Edmonton: Hurtig, 1981), 41–45 and 135–45.

37   Thorstina [Jackson] Walters, *Modern Sagas: The Story of the Icelanders in North America* (Fargo: North Dakota Institute for Regional Studies, 1953), 70 and 1, italics mine.

38   See note 6.

39   Wilfrid Eggleston, *Homestead on the Range* (Ottawa, Canada: Borealis Press, 1982), 39; and Elsie Hammond Diary No. 7, April 27, 1913 and Diary No. 12, July 7, 1915, Elsie Hammond Thomas Papers (hereafter EHTP), Saskatchewan Archives Board-Regina (hereafter SAB-R).

40   My thinking has been influenced by general reading in manuscript and autobiographical sources from the U.S. and Canadian grasslands and by Dan Flores, "Place: An Argument for Bioregional History," *Environmental History Review* 18 (winter 1994): 1–18.

41   Brown, *Sketches*, 40 and 210.

42   Walters, *Modern Sagas*, 13.

43   The story of Jackson's life is interwoven with her study, *Modern Sagas.*

44   Hale Humphrey, Faulkton, Dakota Territory, to Alfred Humphrey, Charles City, Iowa, October 25, 1885, Humphrey Family Papers, South Dakota State Archives, Pierre.

45   Elsie Hammond Diary No. 14, "Geography" school notes follow the April 25, 1916 entry, EHTP, SAB-R.

46   Annora Brown, *Old Man's Garden* (Toronto: J. M. Dent & Sons, 1954).

47   Torchy Anderson, review of *Old Man's Garden*, by Annora Brown, *Vancouver Province B.C. Magazine* (April 17, 1954): 12; and W.G. Stephens, to Annora Brown, Fort Macleod, AB, May 5, 1954, both from Annora Brown Papers, University of Alberta Archives, Edmonton.

48   George F. Will, *Corn for the Northwest* (St. Paul, MN: Webb Book Publishing, 1930), 5, and 10–11; and "Oscar H. Will & Co." Seed Catalog Collection, George Francis Will Papers, North Dakota Institute for Regional Studies Archives, Fargo.

Chapter 8

Fort Macleod of the Borderlands: Using the Forty-Ninth Parallel on Southern Alberta's Ranching Frontier[1]

Peter S. Morris, Santa Monica College

Gordon Burton (1916–1990), the late ranching "perfessor" of southwestern Alberta's Porcupine Hills and former President of the Western Stock Growers' Association, was a true product of the Canadian-American borderlands.[2] Beyond the simple fact that he sojourned in the United States long enough to earn a Ph.D. in agricultural economics from Iowa State University, Dr. Burton's was a life that spanned both sides of the forty-ninth parallel. Like many of his Alberta neighbours, he was the product of a mixed marriage: his mother was from Oregon and his father was from Ontario, a binational parentage which belies the double meaning of the phrase, "Canadian-American relations."[3] But closer inspection of Burton's family history reveals an international border that was more than simply an imaginary line. Indeed, one might reasonably describe the forty-ninth parallel as one of the instrumental forces that brought his parents together on Canada's southwestern plains.

There were, of course, other forces at work, and none was more important than the westering spirit, which captured the dreams and imaginations of so many North Americans in the nineteenth century. Burton's mother, Minnie

Furman, had been raised in Baker City, Oregon, where her parents had relocated from New York state in the early 1850s. Burton's father, Frederick, moved west as a young man, leaving in 1886 his parents' modest Ontario home at the age of eighteen. He first hired on with the Winder Ranche, located northwest of Fort Macleod, but soon decided to go "into business for himself," squatting on a "timbered well-grassed coulee" on the Winder's 50,000-acre lease. The existence of this Dominion lease, and the government's feeble attempts to move Burton off the land to make way for what it termed "serious ranchers," made his a distinctively Canadian western experience. His efforts were shortly rewarded, though, with both a homestead and a pre-emption tract of land, and this property became the seed of the home ranch that he and Minnie would subsequently create. In short, the Burtons' is a story not unfamiliar to denizens of Frederick Jackson Turner's "American" West.

The Burtons' story, though, is more than simply a transnational tale of Ontario boy meets Oregon girl on the North American frontier. In fact, central to their story is that pre-eminent symbol of Canadian nationalism, the North West Mounted Police (NWMP). The Winder Ranche Company was formed in 1880 under the direction of Captain William Winder, the NWMP superintendent whose boosting of the grazing lands around Fort Macleod while on leave in Quebec, did much to generate eastern interest in large-scale Canadian ranching.[4] The NWMP, in other words, provided both an inspirational magnet and an institutional foundation that drew young Canadian men such as Frederick Burton to the southern Alberta foothills.

The NWMP also drew Minnie Furman's family to Canada's southwestern plains. In 1882, Minnie's father and brother trailed horses from their home on the Great Columbia Plain,[5] across the Rocky Mountains, to Fort Benton, Montana, and on to the upper branches of the Saskatchewan. It was a logical transformation of their Columbia River freighting business, which had lately suffered from competition with the railroads. The North West's new Mounted Police, after all, remained isolated from eastern Canada, and they consequently provided a profitable customer for remounts and other livestock and goods imported from across the line. Within four years, the entire Furman family had relocated to the Benton area, and two years later they took a Canadian homestead on the aptly named Boundary Creek. Most of the Furmans would soon return to the United States and a horse ranch in Montana, but not before

Minnie and Frederick had married and another Canadian-American family had been born.

In this brief overview of the Burton family story, we see the enigmatic workings of the forty-ninth parallel. Like all political boundaries, the one between the western United States and Canada is artificial, the work of human beings. Its simple curvilinear form has made this artificiality immediately apparent, in contrast to so-called natural boundaries along rivers, mountain chains, and the like, which tend to obscure the no-less-potent role of human society in defining and enforcing such limits.[6] The forty-ninth parallel boundary's obvious artificiality, combined with the great similarities between Anglophone Canadian and American cultures, have helped make this a highly permeable line, easily crossed by family trees and economic endeavours. Permeability, though, does not necessarily translate into insignificance, and the presence of the border would significantly shape the region's development. The border provided an important legal divide, a territorial division in jurisdiction and political-economic authority. The border also divided the region between two distinctive national contexts which, among other things, stimulated the creation of federal institutions such as the NWMP to secure each half of the region for its respective country. And perhaps most importantly, the border shaped how this region came to be understood. Whatever unity and similarity might transcend the forty-ninth parallel, one side carries the labels of Canada and Alberta, while the other side is known to the world as Montana and the United States. Each of these names carries with them a unique set of ideas and images, and this simple difference in language makes these two halves of the northwestern plains two different places.[7] This essay explores these multiple dimensions of the forty-ninth parallel boundary as they emerged in and around southwestern Alberta's Fort Macleod during the first quarter century of its existence.

AMERICAN OUTPOST IN THE CANADIAN WEST

Fort Macleod was born when three of the six troops constituting the new NWMP arrived on the banks of the Oldman River in October 1874.[8] Despite a modest first impression,[9] the NWMP quickly became a highly efficient and effective force and a potent national symbol. In now-legendary fashion with surprisingly little violence, the Police ended the illegal Montana-based whisky trade, which had been flourishing north of the border for the previous five years, by shutting down operations at the region's notorious trading posts – transient places with colourful names such as Whoop-Up, Standoff, and Slide-Out. In the words of American historian Paul Sharp, "Whoop-Up country so changed in character with the entry of the police that the name itself fell into disuse." Fort Macleod, in short, became the epicentre of the Canadianization of the northwestern plains.[10]

The small settlement that grew up around the fort, however, developed as a remarkably American place. Without a Canadian steamboat or rail connection, the police depended heavily on merchants in Montana for supplies and services – everything from the Christmas turkey to watch repair. Even as the police were constructing their fort in the late autumn of 1874, the Fort Benton-based company of I. G. Baker constructed a trading post right next door; in addition to supplying the troops with more than $23,000 worth of beef and cattle during the first four seasons alone, Baker and Co. became the NWMP's official banker in charge of distributing its payroll. Other Benton merchants, such as John Glenn, Thomas C. Power, and Tony LaChappelle, would soon join Baker to participate in this lucrative beyond-the-end-of-the-railroad trade, and Americans would play a prominent role in the district's affairs for the next fifteen years. Even the locally famous Macleod school bell originally adorned a Missouri River steamer. Rather than eliminating American influence in this corner of the Canadian West, the NWMP simply transformed it into a legal and legitimate affair.[11]

No man better personifies this transformation than D. W. Davis. Born in Vermont in 1845, and wounded eighteen years later at Gettysburg, Davis arrived in the northwestern plains in 1867 as a quartermaster sergeant at Montana's Fort Shaw. Within three years, Davis had left the U.S. Army and was working for the infamous whisky-trading partnership of Healy and Hamilton, running a small post in the vicinity of present-day Calgary. In 1874, he was in charge, but not present, when the NWMP arrived at Fort Whoop-Up to shut down its illegal business. This turn of events was more an opportunity than a threat, however, and Davis became I. G. Baker's resident general manager at Macleod. In the meantime, Davis participated in the 1880s ranching boom by raising NWMP remounts with his partner Frank Strong; he became a naturalized British subject; he organized the Macleod Improvement Company serving as its first president; and in 1887 he defeated former Hudson's Bay Company (HBC) factor Richard Hardisty to become the District of Alberta's first Member of Parliament in Ottawa.[12] Even his latter-day detractors thus recognize Davis as an early "pillar of the community of Fort Macleod," and his legacy would live on well into the twentieth century; in 1939, his son G. Rider Davis began an eighteen-year tenure as the town's mayor.[13]

D. W. Davis thus was a borderland Janus, facing south as a quintessential frontiersman from the wild American West and facing north as a central figure in the mythically tame civilization of the Canadian West. Like many of his contemporaries, Davis could not fully escape the stigma of having participated in the whisky trade. His family remembers him as "an intelligent, even tempered man ... courteous and hospitable ... hardly the qualities attributed to a whiskey trader." But his frontier-American past fits uneasily within the national Canadian epic of securing a kindler, gentler, more civilized West from invasive U.S. interests. For example, his 1887 election to the Dominion Parliament was tainted by rumours that he had bribed constituents with whisky smuggled into the North-West via the bladders of a sleigh-load of hog carcasses. Such stories, truthful or not, have underlain many a heroic legend of the American frontier, and been as much the source of praise for pragmatic grit and individualism as the source of condemnation for lawlessness and incivility. Such praise is less likely offered in a Canadian context, however, and Davis's most recent Canadian biographer instead described him as a man with "little sympathy for any interests other than his own." Quite simply, "one cannot view Davis as a Canadian hero."[14] Passing judgment on any individual's life is notoriously difficult, particularly when attempting to do so across the great distance between past and present. Rather than to second or to challenge this unfavourable assessment of Davis, I wish to present it simply as an illustration of how the forty-ninth parallel has shaped our understanding of the region and its inhabitants – how the same local and regional stories fit differently, and thus take on different meanings, in the two national contexts.

The completion of the Canadian Pacific's main line across the Alberta plains in 1883 is appropriately viewed as a pivotal event in the reorientation of the borderlands surrounding Macleod onto a new all-Canadian axis. Less than a decade later, the most prominent American firm in Macleod, I. G. Baker and Co., sold its Canadian holdings to the HBC. With the concurrent rise of Canada's distinctive leasehold ranching system, which was dominated in the southwestern Alberta foothills by British and Anglo-Canadian owners, Canadian national society and culture took firm hold of the region. According to the historian Andy den Otter:

> Although the ... Fort Benton companies dominated commerce in southern Alberta for two decades, their cultural legacy is minimal.... The ranchers and NWMP officers formed the region's elite and their values dominated its society.[15]

This Canadianization of the southern Alberta plains, however, was gradual and incomplete. The historical geographer Simon Evans has detailed the many important American inputs into Canadian ranching. In addition to the presence of numerous U.S.-based ranches outside of the elite foothills region, the large British- and Canadian-owned ranches were stocked primarily with American cattle and operated by largely American labour and know-how.[16] As a visiting London journalist reported in November 1886:

> The foremen, herders and cowboys are mostly from the States. In fact, this district, its towns and manners and methods are very American, so that it seems much like a section of the western American frontier.[17]

As the era of the large ranches succumbed in the 1890s to the same homestead-settlement pressures that dealt a deathblow to open-range ranching south of the line, American ties to the Macleod district remained strong. Agricultural settlement of the North-West could not take place without significant immigration, and white American settlers were highly desired.[18] In 1909, a visiting German journalist writing from Calgary reported that, "In Canada, the government and the people consider the Americans to be by far the most welcome settlers;" not only did they come equipped with a good supply of initial capital, thanks in large part to gains on land sold at high prices in the

American Middle West, but they generally possessed "experience with farming under similar conditions."[19]

This last point was particularly salient for the arid plains of southern Alberta, where experience with irrigation and dry farming was highly coveted. It took no more than a year, for example, for the refugee Latter-day Saints of Cache Valley, Utah, led by Charles Ora Card, to feel welcome at their new home on Lee's Creek, south of Macleod. Initial Canadian concerns regarding their possible importation of Mormon polygamy led Card in June 1887 to advise his "brethren and sisters to be guarded in their sayings before strangers." By the following February, however, Card was happily recording in his diary that he "chatted quite freely" in Macleod with the local Collector of Customs, who said "he had recd [*sic*] instructions from the Government that he was to do all he could to encourage our people to settle in this country which he intended to do." Card also noted that Macleod's postmaster and sheriff, Duncan Campbell, "has always been on hand to aid us all he could and being a man of extended information has been a help to me in various ways."[20]

The historian Bruce Shepard recently compiled a variety of statistics on the national origins of Canadian immigration. Between 1909 and 1912, the peak of western Canada's settlement boom, 28 per cent of the homestead entries were filed by U.S. citizens – more than any other citizenship group, including Canadians. During the same period, fully three- quarters of Canada's 268,000 immigrants were U.S. citizens, as were two-thirds of all the Canadian Pacific Railway's land customers registered at Calgary. As a result, Americans became "the largest foreign nationality to farm the Canadian Plains," and, along with the British and native-born Canadians, one of the three national groups that, in Shepard's words, "dominated the population of the region."[21]

USING THE BORDER

For all of these American inputs and connections, however, the Macleod district and the rest of the Canadian plains remained a distinctive place. The region's Amerindian populations notwithstanding, the forty-ninth parallel was for the majority of residents an "antecedent boundary" – a line placed on the map well before they arrived in the region.[22] At a minimum, the border shaped preconceptions of the regional environment. For example, William Howell McIntyre, Sr., a Texas-born rancher from Utah, received glowing reports of the grazing lands of southwestern Alberta from a friend who had recently returned from the Mormon settlements at Cardston. Despite being in a desperate search for new land, given the poor condition at that time of the ranges in Utah and Wyoming – not exactly places of balmy climates themselves – McIntyre waited four years to even visit Alberta. According to a family memoir:

> The Name Canada immediately conjured up thoughts of long, cold winters in his imagination, and consequently he determined to give Canada a long look before making any permanent move towards locating in that country.

Three years of investigations later, his concerns were finally eased and the McIntyre Ranch became one of the leading operations along Pot Hole Creek, on the north side of the Milk River Ridge.[23] But preconceptions about the comparative qualities of the U.S. and Canadian plains did not always disappear upon arrival in the region. In fact, these ideas could shape one's perceptions of the area, colouring the landscape for the viewer in distinctive national shades. As is discussed in greater detail below, this was particularly true when nation-based ideas resonated with motives regarding land use and settlement.

More than just a passive frame for regional ideas, the forty-ninth parallel boundary has been actively used by area residents. As is true in border regions everywhere, many have sought to exploit the opportunities presented by this line of transition in legal jurisdiction. For some, this involved smuggling, such as the infamous northward flow of contraband whisky into Canada during the "Whoop-Up" era, which would later be matched by a similar flow of booze southward during U.S. Prohibition in the 1920s. But smuggling was not limited to illegal alcohol. Beginning in 1882, for example, immigration restrictions into the United States offered smugglers such as Gus Brede the lucrative option of directing a southward flow of Chinese labourers across the line. In his annual report for 1891, the commanding officer at Fort Macleod, Samuel Steele, described Brede as "a thorn in the side of the police." Despite repeated arrests and heavy fines, "nothing seemed to daunt him" – at least not until Mother Nature stepped in and struck Brede that summer with a bolt of lightning while on the trail to Benton. Thus ended one smuggler's career, but it hardly sealed this most porous of international boundaries.[24]

Several of the region's residents instead have sought to smuggle themselves across the border. This is particularly true of people who have found themselves outside the law in either country, many of whom have attempted to cross this "Medicine Line"[25] and thus use the border as momentary refuge from authorities. Some of these borderland refugees are famous – Sitting Bull, Louis Riel, Charles Card and his Mormon brethren – but they are joined by many others whose names are not so well-known. For example, it was not uncommon for deserters from both the U.S. Army and Canada's Mounted Police to seek refuge on the other side. Long before it became a modern, border-crossing highway, the Wild Horse route between Havre, Montana, and Medicine Hat, Alberta, was commonly used by American "Buffalo Soldiers" deserting Fort Assinniboine. In the opposite direction, the NWMP commander for the Lethbridge-based "K" Division reported five desertions in one year alone, with four successfully escaping into the States. One of these deserters did so rather mundanely, while on a one-month pass to Ottawa; another made a more dramatic midnight escape on horseback, and then on foot southward beyond the Milk River.[26]

Counted among this borderland's many refuge-seeking outlaws also was the apparently ubiquitous population of horse- and cattle-thieves. Today's national mythologies posit a "wild" American West against a peaceful, orderly, law-abiding Canadian West. Whatever merit this contrast might have as a gross generalization, however, should not hide from us a more complicated reality. Neither country held a monopoly on outlaws attempting to escape to the other side, including those of the Wild West livestock-rustler kind. Nor did crossing the Medicine Line provide outlaws with a magical get-out-of-jail-free card; whether it was north or south of the forty-ninth parallel, freedom from justice was often short-lived.

The case of the Canadian outlaw Edward "The Kid" Austin provides a useful illustration. In November 1888, the NWMP suspected Austin of the theft of a horse, bridle, and overcoat belonging to Tom Purcel of Milk River Ridge in present-day Alberta. Austin fled southward across the border and sought refuge on a Montana ranch, only to be seized by those ranchers when they learned of his alleged crime north of the border. His guilt apparently confirmed by a subsequent attempt to re-steal Purcel's horse and saddle, Austin readily submitted to Canadian authorities when presented with the option, rather than face the prospect of an informal justice handed out by the Montana ranchers. According to the NWMP's district superintendent, R. Burton Deane, this was the obvious choice: "he was doubtless right in conjecturing that his shrift would be short if he prolonged his stay on the southern side of the international boundary." Austin's story testifies both to the interconnectedness of the Canadian and American plains as well as to their differences; Austin fled to U.S. territory because it was outside Canadian jurisdiction, but when his chance for refuge disappeared, he returned to Canada to face what was perceived to be a less capricious system of justice.[27]

Use of the border went beyond attempts to evade legal authority, and the border became an integral tool in efforts to control access to the region's resources. Early Canadian ranching interests sought to use the border to protect their investment in purebred bulls and heifers, as well as their exclusive rights to the southern Alberta range. This they did by lobbying for quotas, tariffs, and quarantines against imported cattle, and by attempting to mobilize the NWMP on their behalf to patrol the borderland range against livestock straying northward across the line in search of forage (even as they allowed their own animals to stray southward into the United States). With greater subtlety, foothills ranchers – such as those who met in Macleod in November 1886 to form the Canadian North-West Territories Stock Association – also used the border's presence to neatly frame their arguments for increased government protection of their range:

> Your memorialists represent all the practical stock owners of this country.... They are conscious that, in so doing, they are contributing not only to the protection of an important industry, but are taking a material part in preserving to Canada the last and best stock range on the Continent, the loss of which would be recognized, when too late, as a national disaster.[28]

The allegedly poor condition of the Montana range at this time was as much a product of perception as of reality. The northern borderlands of Montana were not heavily stocked until the late 1890s, after the arrival of the Great Northern Railroad. Nonetheless, as a part of entities known as "Montana" and the "United States," the northern Montana range was readily associated with the truly poor conditions in the 1880s found elsewhere on the American plains and the earlier-claimed lands of central and southeastern Montana. Natural climate fluctuations also played a significant role as the 1886 summer had been a notoriously dry one, preceding the infamous 1886–87 winter that led to widespread herd losses throughout the North American plains. The infancy of western Canadian ranching allowed the CNWTSA delegates meeting in Macleod to dismiss that winter's difficulties as a distinctly American tragedy, but range conditions north of the line do not appear to have been much better. Indeed, during the preceding summer, American ranchers hoping to find greener Canadian pastures for their cattle were sharply disappointed. In July, Daniel Marsh informed his Montana-based partner, Thomas Power, "In coming from Winnipeg west I find the country all dried up grass very short and water scarce, particularly in the Maple Creek country." Indeed, Marsh continued:

> If you enter stock for your range this summer, unless rain falls, think you will have to let the cattle drift south across the boundary after you have secured the free entry for them at Maple Creek.[29]

At once, Marsh reminds us in these words that while the border was a tangible legal presence, its effectiveness at controlling the movement of livestock (not to mention the rain and snow or lack thereof) was limited. In fact, despite repeated efforts during the 1890s and early 1900s to limit cattle drifting across the border, including proposals to fence its length, the "Last Great Roundup" in 1907 remained an international affair, with ranchers' reps from both sides of the line participating in co-operation.[30]

For the CNWTSA memorialists, though, the *de facto* permeability of the forty-ninth parallel border to man, beast, and the elements, was largely irrelevant. It certainly did not make the border any less usable for their political purposes. By pointing to a proximately located bad example from another country, Canadian ranchers were able to argue that theirs was a case of vital *national* interest. The border not only framed their argument – don't let what happened to *their* range happen to *our* range – but the border gave their cause larger geographical significance that Ottawa, it was hoped, could not ignore.

DUNCAN MCEACHRAN AND THE NEW WALROND RANCHE

The experiences of the prominent Macleod-area rancher Duncan McEachran illustrate the many ways in which the forty-ninth parallel border could be used. A native of Scotland, McEachran visited Canada's southwestern prairies for the first time in 1881, seven years after the NWMP made their legendary march to the West. After graduating from Edinburgh's Dick's Veterinary College, which later became incorporated into the Royal Veterinary College, McEachran moved to Quebec and became a prominent figure among the Anglo stock raisers of the Eastern Townships, across the river from Montreal. Then, following nearly two decades in eastern Canada, he travelled west in 1881 to take his position as the resident manager of the new Cochrane Ranche, located in the foothills above Fort Calgary. Earlier that year, McEachran and Senator Matthew Henry Cochrane – also of Montreal – had successfully lobbied for a new grazing-lease policy in the North-West Territories. And by no coincidence, the first of these 100,000-acre leases was awarded to the newly formed ranching company of which Cochrane and McEachran were the leading shareholders.[31]

As was standard practice at the time, McEachran reached Canada's southwestern plains by way of the Missouri River and its head of navigation at Fort Benton. These were the waning days of what the historian Paul Sharp has described as "Whoop-Up Country," a period of transition between the departure of the HBC and the arrival of the Canadian Pacific Railway, during which Fort Benton served as this borderland region's de facto commercial centre.[32] Travelling overland north from Benton, McEachran recorded his observations at length for publication back home in the *Montreal Gazette*.[33]

Two themes are prominent in these observations. First, McEachran makes a number of unexceptional comments regarding the strangeness of this distant frontier, noting, for example, the "mixed" population at Benton, with its menagerie of general merchants only one step removed from the old fur trade. He also describes the "grand sight" of eight massive wagon trains on their way between Benton and Canada's western plains' outposts, each drawn by a team of sixteen "fine working" oxen. As for the treeless grassland landscape itself, he described it as "a great waste of land, level as far as eye could see." McEachran had crossed the border all right – the Turnerian border between eastern civilization and the western frontier.[34]

McEachran, though, also found significance in the other border he was crossing, the forty-ninth parallel boundary between Canada and the United States. That the route between Canada proper and its newly acquired North-West ran through the United States was at least mildly unsettling to McEachran. While at Macleod, for example, McEachran found he had to send his domestic mail south of the line:

> We here wrote and mailed several letters to our dear ones at home, but, anomalous as it may seem, we found that in the Dominion of Canada, at a Dominion post office, Canadian postage stamps were of no use, and we had to frank our letters with American postage stamps.[35]

Moreover, like others both before and after him, McEachran's personal views of the region and its landscapes were clearly shaped and framed by this antecedent political boundary. He praised the early work of the NWMP, whose "successful management" of the Blackfoot Indians offered a "marked contrast to the trouble and discontent" among the Indians living south the line.[36]

More than just government policy, however, distinguished the lands north and south of the forty-ninth parallel in McEachran's eyes. In fact, the difference seems to have been instilled by Nature itself. McEachran writes:

> A short distance from our camp we passed the boundary line, and, strange as it may seem, we felt that we were more at home [and] wished we had a Union Jack to wave above us…. No sooner did we enter the Dominion than a most marked improvement was at once observable in the soil and the pasture, an improvement which continued to increase till we reached our destination at the Bow River.[37]

However distinctive any contrasts between the two sides of the line may or may not actually have been – and it's doubtful there was much of a contrast given the extremely low population densities and open-range grazing practices on both sides of the line at the time – this antecedent boundary clearly shaped the way McEachran viewed the region and its landscapes. Since these comments were written for public consumption, we must take them with a grain of salt. They likely are a reasonably fair summary of what McEachran actually believed, but they also were part of a concerted campaign to preserve Canada's southwestern plains, and in particular Alberta's foothills district, for the emerging elite ranching community of which McEachran was a part. And as the next few decades would show, the border between the United States and Canada provided him with an important tool in those preservation efforts.

McEachran did not remain long with the Cochrane Ranche. By 1883, just two years after his initial trip to the region, he had recruited the capital of British Conservative Sir John Walrond-Walrond to form what would become the North-West Territories' largest cattle operation by the end of the decade.[38] With offices in Montréal, McEachran served as General Manager of the Walrond Ranche Co., whose 260,000 acres of grazing leases were located near Pincher Creek, in the shadow of the Crowsnest Pass west of Fort Macleod. McEachran would go on to manage the company until his retirement in ill health in 1923.[39]

Would-be cattle barons such as McEachran were drawn to the Canadian West by a happy coincidence of circumstances during the 1870s. The "opening" of the Canadian plains through the near-extermination of the northern bison herds and the dispossession of Blackfoot Indian lands, provided both a vast supply of rich grazing lands and a sizeable local market for beef at the region's new Indian reserves, the supervising NWMP posts, and the soon-to-follow construction camps and towns of the Canadian Pacific Railway. Meanwhile, the decimation of British and continental-European cattle herds by disease provided a potentially lucrative export market for North American beef. But the full realization of this potential "beef bonanza" rested on two things – the genetic quality and health of the livestock and the quality of the range itself.[40] In seeking to preserve both of these things, McEachran and his colleagues relied heavily on the forty-ninth parallel boundary and the Dominion government's willingness to enforce it.

Like his former partner Senator Cochrane, McEachran invested heavily in the genetic resources of the Walrond Ranche's livestock. While most of the initial "stocker" cattle were imported from Montana and the Great Columbia Plain – duty-free under the terms of their government lease agreements – it was the job of several dozen purebred bulls from Ontario and Britain to "gradually raise the quality" of the Walrond's herds.[41] It was thus imperative to protect this large capital investment from potential invasions from south of the border – invasions both genetic and pathogenic. The latter of these two American threats was particularly significant since, in 1878, the British House of Lords proposed a ban on live cattle imports to protect their country's herds from further decimation. Only through measures such as the 1879 Quarantine Act were Canadian ranches able to retain access to the British beef market for the next dozen years.[42]

Dr. McEachran, Canada's chief stock inspector from 1884 to 1902, played a central role in these Canadian disease-prevention efforts. As early as 1875, he had lobbied the Dominion government for a quarantine system to protect Canadian livestock. This quarantine service was reorganized under McEachran's lead in 1884, when a pleuro-pneumonia outbreak in the Midwestern states posed a potential new threat to newly established ranches such as the Walrond. Fort Macleod, located only a few dozen miles down the Oldman River from the Walrond's lands, was made a veterinary import inspection point; three years later, McEachran was able to erect an even stronger boundary, successfully lobbying for a ninety-day quarantine of cattle imported from the United States, with the reservation of a twelve-mile-deep strip of land along the north side of the border to serve as a quarantine grazing district. Since McEachran's Walrond Ranche was one of the primary beneficiaries of his securing the border as Dominion stock inspector, he not surprisingly became the target of various conflict-of-interest charges made by small ranchers and early homesteaders; some were upset specifically with the quarantine, others more generally with the virtual fiefdom the large cattle operations had been able to secure through their access to capital and their government leases.[43]

In addition to protecting their livestock, McEachran and his colleagues actively sought to use the forty-ninth parallel boundary to protect the animals' rangeland sustenance. To a certain extent, the border was a direct shield against possible encroachment from American ranchers. Especially, as the open-range lands in southern and central Montana became widely overgrazed during the 1880s, many south of the border saw the relatively untouched grasslands of western Canada as a possible refuge. For example, the manager of the Powder River Cattle Company reported to his superiors in 1885, "our one chance of safety and of future profit, lay in a rapid removal to the leased ranges north of the British line."[44] But perhaps even more importantly, the forty-ninth parallel provided a rhetorical boundary with which McEachran and others sought to mobilize the resources of the Dominion government against a foe – small ranchers and homesteaders such as Frederick Burton – that was largely of domestic, Canadian origin.[45]

Throughout the relatively short fifteen-year history of the large grazing leases in southern Alberta, the British-Canadian interests who controlled the foothills region made frequent use of the American situation to bolster their claims for government protection against homesteaders and squatters. For example, in October 1886, McEachran and other representatives from neighbouring ranches petitioned the Interior Minister to provide and protect special hay and water reserves and for a new 50 per cent import duty on all livestock not belonging to government leaseholders. A few weeks later, many of the same men participated in the Macleod meeting of the CNWTSA that warned Ottawa of an imminent "national disaster" – the potential degradation of "the last and best stock range on the Continent," which in the absence of "immediate measures" is destined to be "rendered valueless" by the "same causes that have destroyed the stock ranges of the adjoining American states."[46]

The Interior Department's response to the ranchers' 1886 petitions made apparent that the underlying threats to the territorial integrity of the foothills grazing leases came less from some sort of American invasion and more from the growing presence of Canadian homesteaders and squatters. In an internal memorandum to Minister Thomas White, Deputy Minister A. M. Burgess commented favourably on the ranchers' proposal to modify current regulations concerning stocking density. But he also revealed the Dominion government's inability – and unwillingness – to protect the large-lease ranches from anything more than isolated individual squatters:

> when an actual settler desires the land for the purpose of making his home upon it, it would be impossible, even if it were expedient, to keep him out. It is not meant by this that one or two speculative settlers should be allowed to disturb a whole grazing ranche, but when the wave of settlement reaches the confines of the grazing country, if that country be found fit for the purpose of actual settlement, it will in my humble opinion be impossible to maintain it for purely grazing purposes.[47]

Burgess made it clear that the government would do all it could to protect the integrity of "individual property" in the North-West Territories. But that did not mean the government would be willing to stand in the way of the advancement of Canada's own agricultural settlement frontier.

No individual leasehold rancher was more personally involved in the conflict with incoming homesteaders than McEachran. Both his work as Dominion veterinarian to strictly control and limit the importation of livestock, and his diligent, public efforts to protect the Walrond leases from encroachment – efforts described locally as the "Walrond War on Settlers" – made McEachran a marked man. In 1891, he requested assistance from the NWM after a fire destroyed three hundred tons of the ranch's hay; according to McEachran, this alleged act of arson was the "inauguration of a reign of terrorism and lawlessness" by disgruntled settlers shut out of the Walrond's leased lands.[48] Later that same year, the NWMP commander for the Macleod District reported:

> ... a very irritated feeling existing on all sides but more particularly on the part of settlers on the Waldron [sic] Land who seem to entertain a personal hostility towards the Manager Mr. McEachran who they complain is continually threatening them and harassing them, preventing them from cutting hay and refusing employment to any one who owns a hoof of stock in the country.[49]

At one point, McEachran was apparently the target of a disgruntled settler's gunfire, and McEachran subsequently received a personal escort from the Mounties when visiting the area.[50]

Especially after the end of the Conservative party's government in 1896, and the appointment of Clifford Sifton as the Minister of the Interior, there was little McEachran could do to stem the tide of intensive agricultural settlement in southern Alberta. Not long after its passage, the grazing-lease policy in the North-West Territories came under sharp criticism from a mixture of agrarian-settlement and rival ranching interests. Opponents of the policy such as Moreton Frewen, an Englishman then operating a ranch in the United States, described the policy in a letter to Prime Minister Macdonald as an attempt to "lock up this vast district by a handful of sociable ranche-men settled in one small corner." It took only four years for the grazing policy's opponents to win a doubling of the original penny-per-acre lease rates and to make all new leases susceptible to homestead entry. And just six years after that, the grazing lessees received a circular letter from the Department of Interior informing them that their leases would be honoured only through the end of January 1896.[51] During 1899 alone, an estimated one hundred new settlers made homestead entries at the Dominion Lands sub-agency for Pincher Creek, one-third of these entries located in the townships immediately south of the Walrond ranch. Another twenty-five made entries in the Pincher Creek district at the Dominion Lands office in Lethbridge. In addition, the government estimated that two dozen squatters had located in the district, and that as many as 150 more had recently arrived in the area but had yet to set to select and settle on a homestead. While McEachran and others may have sometimes described this as an American invasion of their ranching domain, the majority of these 1899 arrivals were from Great Britain and eastern Canada.[52]

By 1905, it had become apparent to McEachran that the days of the large foothills ranches were numbered. He informed Sir Walrond that the best course for the company would be to develop its land as a "model colony of good agriculturalists"; since the cancellation of its public-lands grazing lease in 1896, the reorganized New Walrond Ranch Company had purchased nearly 38,000 acres, which McEachran optimistically believed could now be sold at a tidy profit. The same land he had described a quarter-century earlier as being too frost-prone for farming, he now said was "unequalled in this the centre of fall wheat growing," worth as much as twenty dollars per acre. Any hope of retaining the New Walrond's ranching operations were removed following the loss of an estimated five thousand cattle during the disastrous winter of 1906–07. Like so many other area ranches during the following "Carrion Spring," as novelist Wallace Stegner would later describe it, the New Walrond sold off its remaining livestock and set on the long process of liquidating its land holdings.[53]

Despite the loss of his primary incentive to keep American settlers out of the region, McEachran retained his nationalistic frame of reference toward Canada's southwestern plains. He encouraged Sir Walrond to sell the company's land en bloc to a colonization-minded British investor such as Lord Strathcona. McEachran said he was:

ambitious to see it peopled not by amateur farmers, but by good experienced men and women, such as would be certain to make this a model colony in every respect and one that will carry the name of Walrond with credit and renown down the centuries – and I would prefer when we go out of business that British people reap the benefits of our struggles and anxieties instead of as my happen it be given over to the Mormon Church or American speculators.[54]

These patriotic plans, however, would soon prove untenable. The next dozen years produced a series of hope-generating speculations, such as the possibility of a great oil field lying under the Walrond's property or that a new railroad connection would rescue the district from its relative isolation. None of these developments panned out, however, and when World War I virtually halted British and Canadian immigration to the region, McEachran cast a more welcoming eye toward the forty-ninth parallel. In the company's annual report for 1916, he informed shareholders – who had not seen a dividend since the company stopped raising cattle in 1907 – that it was "gratifying to find ... that immigration from the United States continues to increase, in spite of the war." Indeed, the company was now carrying on "considerable correspondence ... with American Stock men and Real Estate firms as to selling or leasing the land, and it is intended to advertise judiciously throughout the Western States."[55]

Dr. Duncan McEachran's nationalism had finally outlived its usefulness; it was no match for the boundary-defying force of capitalism. He had once used the international boundary as both a real, legal barrier to American encroachment, and as a symbolic example that he hoped would mobilize the Dominion government's resources in his efforts to preserve an elite ranching domain. But now, despite a deeply felt British imperial patriotism, the New Walrond's mounting losses made it impossible for McEachran to maintain a hostile attitude toward potential settlers from the great Republic to the south. The exclamation point to McEachran's failed plans for an enduring British-Canadian mixed-farming colony north of the forty-ninth parallel finally arrived in 1946, twenty-two years after McEachran's death, when the last of the New Walrond's land holdings were finally sold off, to a man hailing from Las Vegas, Nevada.[56]

CONCLUDING COMMENTS

The career of Duncan McEachran is clearly exceptional, and it would be presumptuous to claim that his experiences along the forty-ninth parallel were representative of most of the region's residents. While a distinguished leader of important colonizing efforts in southwestern Alberta at the end of the nineteenth century, he never made the area his permanent home. He visited the Fort Macleod district only seasonally, retaining his primary office in Montreal before retiring to the Eastern Townships. His life nonetheless testifies to how connected southern Alberta's history has been to the rest of the continent – how the forty-ninth parallel has in no way prevented this from becoming a North American place, rather than a purely Canadian place – while at the same time demonstrating the great importance of that international divide. Before he even stepped foot in the region, the border framed how he would see and come to know the northwestern plains. Like many others both before and after him, never did he question the fact that on one side of this antecedent boundary was British/Canadian territory, while the other belonged to the United States. Rather than accept this territorial division passively, however, he also tried to exploit it to suit his own interests, as well as his vision of what this North American grassland region should become.

Contrary to its simple cartographic form, the forty-ninth parallel boundary between the western United States and Canada cannot be easily described in terms of its significance to the region. The oft-used metaphor of an "imaginary line" is useful in describing the numerous and frequent crossings of this border, both literal and figurative. Yet this so-called imaginary line has, in fact, powerfully shaped the region's human geographies. A largely antecedent boundary, it was instrumental in defining the region's place on individuals' mental maps. In addition, the border both contained and directed government approaches and responses to the region, and in so doing, these governments created a complex of institutional divides which provided a variety of opportunities for extralegal exploitation. And finally, the border's presence was not static, but instead subject to the transforming efforts of local and non-local interests attempting to harness its legal-institutional and rhetorical power.

NOTES

1   Field and archival research for this paper was funded in part by a 1997–98 Canadian Studies Graduate Student Fellowship from the Canadian Embassy. The author gratefully acknowledges this support.

2   Details of Burton's life and family history are taken from Sherm Ewing, ed., *The Range* (Missoula: Mountain Press, 1990), 43–45, 248.

3   Cf. "Canadian-American relations were a frequent topic of conversation in my grandmother's house. There were the Canadian relations and then there were the American relations, who lived mostly in Boston. That's what makes Canadian-American relations somewhat touchy at times: they *are* relatives." Margaret Atwood, "Canadian-American Relations: Surviving the Eighties," in *Second Words: Selected Critical Prose* (Boston: Beacon Press, 1984), 371.

4   David H. Breen, *The Canadian Prairie West*, 11.

5   Donald W. Meinig, *The Great Columbia Plain: A Historical Geography, 1805–1910* (Seattle: University of Washington Press, 1968; reprint, Seattle: University of Washington Press, 1995).

6   Peter Sahlins, "Natural Frontiers Revisited: France's Boundaries Since the Seventeenth Century," *American Historical Review* 95 (December 1990): 1423–51.

7   Yi-Fu Tuan, "Language and the Making of Place," *Annals of the Association of American Geographers* 81 (1991): 684–96. Peter S. Morris, "Regional Ideas and the Montana-Alberta Borderlands," *Geographical Review* 89 (October 1999): 469–90.

8   John Peter Turner, "The History of 'The Force,'" in *Fort Macleod: The Story of the North West Mounted Police*, ed. H. G. Long (Fort Macleod, AB: Fort Macleod Historical Association, 1993), 12–13.

9   One Montana editor viewed the small, tired, poorly equipped force which stumbled into the region as evidence that the Canadian government "did not know the actual needs of its own country." Typescript copy of "The Mounted Police in the North West Territory," *Fort Benton River Press* (April 8, 1885), in Southern Alberta Project, Glenbow-Alberta Archives (Calgary), M456, file 10-160.

10 Sharp, *Whoop-Up Country*. Reprint, Norman: University of Oklahoma Press, 1973), 106. R. C. Macleod, "Canadianizing the West: The North-West Mounted Police as Agents of the National Policy, 1873–1905," in *Essays on Western History*, ed. Lewis H. Thomas (Edmonton: University of Alberta Press, 1976), 101–10.

11 Mary McDonald et al., eds., *Fort Macleod – Our Colorful Past: A History of the Town of Fort Macleod from 1874 to 1924* (Fort Macleod, AB: Fort Macleod History Book Committee, 1977), 22, 53, 93; A. A. den Otter, "Transportation, Trade and Regional Identity in the Southwestern Prairies," *Prairie Forum* 15 (spring 1990): 1–23, 4; Hugh A. Dempsey, "A Mountie's Diary—1875," in *Fort Macleod: The Story of the North West Mounted Police*, ed. H. G. Long (Fort Macleod, AB: Fort Macleod Historical Association, 1993), 48; Dominion of Canada, *Sessional Papers* (1880), vol. 10, no. 67.

12 Biographical Sketch of D. W. Davis by Eloise Davis (2 October 1973), in Donald Watson Davis Family fonds, Glenbow Archives, M304, file 1. Beverley A. Stacey, "D. W. Davis: Whiskey Trader to Politician," *Alberta History* 38 (summer 1990): 1–11.

13 Stacey, "D. W. Davis," 6.

14 Ibid.

15 A. A. den Otter, "Transportation, Trade and Regional Identity," 18.

16 Simon M. Evans, "American Cattlemen on the Canadian Range, 1874–1914," *Prairie Forum* 4 (spring 1979): 121–35; Simon M. Evans, "The Origins of Ranching in Western Canada: American Diffusion or Victorian Transplant?" *Great Plains Quarterly* 3 (spring 1983): 79–91; Simon M. Evans, "Stocking the Canadian Range," *Alberta History* 26 (summer 1978): 1–8.

17 Quoted in W. M. Elofson, "Adapting to the Frontier Environment: The Ranching Industry in Western Canada, 1881–1914," in *Canadian Papers in Rural History*, ed. Donald H. Akenson (Gananoque, ON: Langdale Press, 1992), 318.

18 Paul F. Sharp, "The American Farmer and the 'Last Best West,'" *Agricultural History* 21 (April 1947): 65–75; Paul F. Sharp, "When Our West Moved North," *American Historical Review* 55 (January 1950): 286–300. The "white" adjective is included advisedly. While Canada did actively recruit immigrants from Eastern Europe, who would have at least stretched Victorian notions of a "white" ethnicity, efforts to recruit black Americans from Oklahoma were ended quickly thanks to a racist backlash in the Prairies. R. Bruce Shepard, "The Origins of the Oklahoma Black Migration to the Canadian Plains," *Canadian Journal of History* 23 (April 1988).

19 Wilhelm Cohnstaedt, *Western Canada, 1909: Travel Letters by Wilhelm Cohnstaedt*, trans. Herta Holle-Scherer (Regina, SK.: Canadian Plains Research Center, University of Regina, 1976), 10.

20 Donald G. Godfrey and Brigham Y. Card, eds., *The Diaries of Charles Ora Card: The Canadian Years, 1886–1903* (Salt Lake City: University of Utah Press, 1993), 58, 62.

21 Robert Bruce Shepard, "American Influence on the Settlement and Development of the Canadian Plains" (Ph.D. diss., University of Regina, 1994), 83, 353, 355, 358.

22 Richard Hartshorne, "Suggestions on the Terminology of Political Boundaries [abstract]," *Annals of the Association of American Geographers* 26 (1936): 56–57.

23 William H. "Billy" McIntyre Jr., "A Brief History of the McIntyre Ranch," pamphlet published by the *Lethbridge Herald* (1947), Medicine Hat Museum & Art Gallery Archives, item M83.36.1, 10–12.

24 Report of S. B. Steele, in Dominion of Canada, *Sessional Papers* (1892), vol. 10, no. 15, p. 34.

25 Beth LaDow, *The Medicine Line.* (New York and London: Routledge, 2000).

26 Report of R. B. Deane, in Dominion of Canada, *Sessional Papers* (1892), vol. 10, no. 15, p. 74. The Buffalo Soldiers' desertion route is recalled in the 1948 reminiscence of James Mitchell Jr., Hope Michael, and Hope Johnson, "Down the Years

at Elkwater," typescript (1981), Medicine Hat Museum and Art Gallery Archives, item M.81.9.1, p. 14.

27 William M. Baker, ed., *Pioneer Policing in Southern Alberta: Deane of the Mounties* (Calgary: Historical Society of Alberta, 1993), 26.

28 C. E. D. Wood, Secretary of the CNWT Stock Association, to Minister of Interior, 3 December 1886, in David Breen National Archives Ranching Collection, Glenbow Archives, M3799 (hereafter cited as Breen Ranching Collection), file 24.

29 Marsh to Power, 4 July 1886, T. C. Power Papers, Montana Historical Society, folder 129-6.

30 Katherine Hughes, "The Last Great Roundup," *Alberta Historical Review* 11 (spring 1963): 1–7. On the 1906–7 winter, see Wallace Stegner, *Wolf Willow: A History, a Story, and a Memory of the Last Plains Frontier* (New York: Viking, 1962; reprint, New York: Penguin, 1990), 220–38.

31 William Naftel, "The Cochrane Ranch," *Canadian Historic Sites: Occasional Papers in Archaeology and History* 16 (1977): 87–90, 99. Cochrane and McEachran each purchased a thousand hundred-dollar shares in the new company, together accounting for three-quarters of the 2,700 shares initially subscribed.

32 Sharp, *Whoop-Up Country*. The HBC surrendered Rupert's Land to the British Crown (and subsequently to the new Dominion of Canada) in 1869. The CPR arrived at Calgary in 1883, with the last transcontinental spike driven two years later.

33 Duncan McNab McEachran, "A Journey Over the Plains: From Fort Benton to Bow River and back," Glenbow Archives, M736. This manuscript was published in five parts in the *Montreal Gazette*, November–December 1881.

34 Ibid., 1, 4, 8.

35 Ibid., 16.

36 Ibid., 34–35.

37 Ibid., 11.

38 A government report in 1890 listed an estimated 13,000 head of cattle on the New Walrond Ranche, more than any other lessee and equal to roughly one-eighth of all cattle on the Canadian plains. William Pearce, Superintendent of Mines, to Secretary of Interior, Stock Returns from Ranches in the North West Territories, January 15, 1890, Breen Ranching Collection, file 18.

39 By 1885, McEachran had sold all but a hundred of his shares in the Cochrane Ranche Co. From its inception, McEachran was a leading shareholder and General Manager (with offices in Montreal) of the original Walrond Ranche Ltd., which changed its name in 1887 to Walrond Cattle Ranche Ltd. In 1896, despite having paid an annual dividend of at least 5 per cent every year and "against the advice and opinion of the Canadian shareholders," who owned just one-seventh of the company, Walrond Cattle Ranche was voluntarily liquidated. This was due both to the cancellation of the company's grazing leases, per new Canadian land policy, and to the death of numerous shareholders and the consequent need to liquidate their estates for inheritance. Naftel, "The Cochrane Ranch," 90; Harry A. Tatro, Historic Ranches Survey, 1973, Glenbow Archives (hereafter cited as

Tatro Ranches Survey) M3804, 96; Prospectus, February 26, 1898, New Walrond Ranche Company Ltd. fonds, Glenbow Archives (hereafter cited as New Walrond fonds), M2425; Memorandum by Dr. MacEachran, 1898, New Walrond fonds, M2426.

40   General James S. Brisbin, *The Beef Bonanza, or, How to Get Rich on the Plains* (Norman: University of Oklahoma Press, 1959); Naftel, "The Cochrane Ranch," 83–84.

41   Naftel, "The Cochrane Ranch," 105; According to Simon Evans, even the original stocker cattle were of better-than-average quality, selectively purchased in Montana and Idaho at premium prices. These animals consisted mostly of shorthorn crosses imported from the Oregon country, rather than the famously scrawny Texas longhorns then being trailed into southeastern Montana from the central and southern plains. Evans, "Stocking the Canadian Range."

42   Naftel, "The Cochrane Ranch," 83–84. After pleuro-pneumonia was discovered among cattle imported from Montréal into Scotland, the British government finally added Canada to the list of "scheduled" countries in November 1892, ending the Canada's live-cattle export trade to Britain. Max Foran, "The Politics of Animal Health: The British Embargo on Canadian Cattle, 1892–1932," *Prairie Forum* 23 (1998): 1–17.

43   Naftel, "The Cochrane Ranch," 83–85.

44   Report of the Late Manager of the Powder River Cattle Company, enclosed with letter from F. L. Stimson, manager of the North West Cattle Co., to Dominion Lands Branch, Department of Interior, September 1, 1887, Breen Ranching Collection, file 24.

45   In rather understated fashion, Interior commissioner H. H. Smith noted the developing tension between Canadian pioneer homesteaders and the large ranches in the late 1880s: "the cattle industry in Alberta has, during the past year, been very successful. There is, however, some little conflict between lessees of grazing tracts and settlers who desire homestead entry upon lands which are under lease." Annual Report of the Department of the Interior for the Year 1888, Dominion of Canada, *Sessional Papers* 1889, vol. 12, no. 15, 6–7.

46   M. H. Cochrane et al. to Minister of Interior, October 9, 1886, and C. E. D. Wood, Secretary of the Canadian North-West Territories Stock Association, to Minister of Interior, December 3, 1886, Breen Ranching Collection, file 24.

47   A. M. Burgess to Thomas White, January 9, 1887, Breen Ranching Collection, file 24.

48   McEachran to Fred White, NWMP Comptroller, January 27, 1891, Breen Ranching Collection, file 4.

49   S. B. Steele to NWMP Commissioner, October 17, 1891, Breen Ranching Collection, file 53.

50   Tatro Ranches Survey, 97.

51   Naftel, "The Cochrane Ranch," 80–83.

52 Arthur Edgar Cox, Sub-Agent of Dominion Lands, Pincher Creek, to W. F. Mc-Creary, Commissioner of Immigration, December 15, 1899, Breen Ranching Collection, file 6.

53 Stegner, *Wolf Willow*; McEachran to Walrond, October 21, 1905, New Walrond fonds, M2424; Tatro Ranches Survey, 98–99.

54 McEachran to Walrond, October 21, 1905, New Walrond fonds, M2424.

55 Nineteenth Annual Report of the New Walrond Ranche Company, Ltd., February 1, 1917, New Walrond fonds, M2423.

56 The New Walrond stubbornly held on to most of its land until 1923, when it was finally forced to begin selling it off at volume under "unfavourable conditions" in order to meet $56,000 of outstanding liabilities. By the end of 1922, the New Walrond had amassed a cumulative operating loss of $169,571.64, or 82 per cent of invested capital. Tatro Ranches Survey, 98–99; Twenty-Fifth Annual Report of the New Walrond Ranche Company, Ltd., February 7, 1923, New Walrond fonds, M2423; Letters to Shareholders from C. W. Buchanan, President, February 15, 1923 and April 6, 1923, New Walrond fonds, M2426.

Index